for Denise. . .

Military forces in every age reflect the
societies they are created to defend.

(Louis Morton, in Glatthaar 1985:xiii)

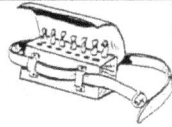

A SKETCH OF THE VIRGINIA SOLDIER IN THE REVOLUTION

Andrew Gallup

HERITAGE BOOKS
2008

HERITAGE BOOKS

AN IMPRINT OF HERITAGE BOOKS, INC.

Books, CDs, and more—Worldwide

For our listing of thousands of titles see our website
at
www.HeritageBooks.com

Published 2008 by
HERITAGE BOOKS, INC.
Publishing Division
100 Railroad Ave. #104
Westminster, Maryland 21157

International Standard Book Number: 978-0-7884-1104-5

CONTENTS

LISTS OF MAPS, ILLUSTRATIONS AND ABBREVIATIONS

LIST OF ABBREVIATIONS
PPS - *Philadelphia Public Store*
PTJ - *Papers of Thomas Jefferson*
VG - *Virginia Gazette*
WGW - *Writings of George Washington*
CVSP - *Calendar of Virginia State Papers*

ACKNOWLEDGEMENTS

Years before I was convinced that a university education, much less a graduate degree, was possible, I was astounded to find that the material was available to build a replica of a flintlock rifle. This reawakened a childhood interest in early American history that has grown to be a major part of my life. Although much of the thrill that the historical mythology instilled in me has vanished, I suppose that the efforts of Fess Parker ought to be acknowledged. Add to this list Kenneth Roberts, John Brick, Bruce Lancaster, King Vidor, and maybe a hundred more responsible for "ripping good adventure yarns."

A couple of years of frustration saw the flintlock rifle finally ready for powder and ball. This led me to a "shoot" the results of which convinced me that there is no genetic link to the ability of your marksman ancestor. Although I could not hit a barn door, this event led me through another door into a world where early American history became interwoven (tangled) with the present day. On that day I met Donald "Doc" Shaffer, my coauthor on an earlier book and co-conspirator on a thousand other projects. This acquaintance, now in its twenty-fourth year, led to participation in various living history programs including depicting the American Revolution, the seed of this book. Resources shared with other reenactors become confused but I am sure Doc, Jim Lynch, Elwood Vaughn, Harry Titus, Greg Novak, Bill Burke, Greg Holms, Dennis Farmer, Tom Edwards and members of the Northwest Territory Alliance had an influence on this work.

In more recent times, many members of the faculty of the Department of Anthropology, The College of William and Mary, deserve mention. Despite my growling, Dr. Ted Reinhart and Dr. Norman Barka did great service, with great patience, although the entire faculty had influence, indeed, indeed. I must remember my fellow graduate students, especially Richard Pougher who provided a source of argument, often Chicago-style, which no one, aside from us, understood.

Finally, my wife, Denise, must be mentioned. She is the one who convinced me that higher education, even for an old guy, was possible. She has been understanding, or at least has appeared so, for the last twenty years and for this I am grateful. Perhaps someday she will understand the difference between procrastination and the artists' mood.

AG

INTRODUCTION

The nucleus of this study, the equipment of the Virginia foot soldier in the American Revolution, was gathered for the author's masters thesis, "The Equipment of the Virginia Soldier in the Revolution." The thesis presented the argument, *if military forces do reflect the society they are created to defend, and material culture is a reflection of the society that created it, then military material culture will reflect the military mindset of the society.* The thesis concluded that the material culture studied suggested that the early United States had a non-militaristic culture.

The military of the American Revolution was chosen for study as it represented an important group in a formative period of a national character, an American identity. The Virginians were chosen as they assumed a leadership role for the southern region of the United States during the war. This was similar to Massachusetts in the north and, like Massachusetts, Virginians played critically important roles in military and nonmilitary affairs during the formative years of the new republic.

An important theme in the thesis argument was that the equipment used by the American soldier usually was simple and functional (simple, here, meaning lack of decorative features). This is, of course, in comparison to his British and German adversaries and other eighteenth-century European military forces. Lack of decoration was partly the result of well documented economic problems facing the colonial governments. Yet, even in later prosperous times, fancy American military uniforms were passing fads, usually the product of a strong, and often wealthy, local military leader. Seldom were ornate uniforms seen in the national army.

Economic problems were only one of many cultural components to have a role in the design of the equipment. One of these components is religion. The Revolution had a strong religious undertone. This undoubtedly had an impact on the form of the material culture of the period. Historian Edmund S. Morgan believes that the religious aspects of early American culture had a primary effect on the American Revolution:

> Without pretending to explain the whole variety of the Revolution, I should like to suggest that the movement in all its phases, from the resistance against Parliamentary taxation in the 1760's to the establishment of a national government and national policies in the 1790's was affected, not to say guided, by a set of values inherited from the age of Puritanism (Morgan 1968:236).

Morgan interprets the Puritan Ethic as a value system based on every man being called by God to serve Him, society, and himself, in a productive manner. A man should also be thrifty. These values would cause a distrust of the idle rich and merchants: the former because they did not produce or serve, and the latter because they were seen to overcharge for their services (Morgan 1968:236-237). As the nobility and the merchant class represented the power behind England's repressive policies, it is not surprising that the colonists developed a distrust of the mother country.

This value system was strongest among the Congregationalists of New England, however, leading Anglicans in the southern colonies, such as Henry Laurens and Richard Henry Lee, demonstrated agreement, as did deists, Franklin and Jefferson (Morgan 1968:239). The religious revival of the mid-eighteenth century had a strong enough effect on Anglican Virginia to create a "party spirit" in the politics of the colony (Heimert 1978:437).

A divine mandate demanding frugality and avoidance of extravagance would greatly affect the material culture. This would be amplified by the boycott movements preceding the Revolution. Boycotts, designed to repeal British tax laws, included artisans wearing leather work clothes (rather than English-made cloth or clothing), students refusing to drink beer, an avoidance of mutton to increase wool supplies, and in the case of the Stamp Act, a boycott of all British goods (Morgan 1968:240).

These nonimportation boycotts, in the opinion of some, renewed ancestral values. It also spurred a movement toward self-sufficiency. Abigail Adams wrote that she would work with her hands. Although the movement toward industry fell short of providing the production necessary to totally supply the war effort, it did instill a belief that the colonists could provide their own manufactured goods. They were developing a sense of political and economic independence (Morgan 1968:241, 245, 251).

Frugality and avoidance of extravagance are readily recognizable characteristics of the military material culture discussed in this study. The economic condition of the United States had an effect on the form of this equipment as did religious/ethical beliefs. The idea that the equipment reflects the society's attitude toward militarism and war is compatible with these cultural forces. The attitude of the eighteenth-century American toward war was a product of the same belief system that preached frugality:

> According to American ministers, war was a sin and a product of sin. God permitted it and guided it for the improvement of His people. In practice, this meant that Britons sinned in waging war, while Americans suffered the consequences of war because of their own sins... (Royster 1979:13).

If a system of religious/ethical beliefs dictated a purpose to war, would not the economy and frugality concerning material culture contained in that system be part of the war effort? If the war effort is successful it is because of God's guidance and this guidance justifies the cause. The material culture of the Virginia soldier shows frugality especially when compared to the extravagance found in the nonfunctional decorative attributes of European equipment. The success of the American cause is partly due to the equipment that made victory possible.

This work will present, and be limited to, the basic equipment used by the infantryman from Virginia who served with the Continental Army during the War of Independence.

This includes his uniform, weapon and other items of common equipment. Particular attention will be given to those articles that can be documented in primary sources. Much less time will be spent speculating on what might have been used. Also absent in this work are common items of daily life, i.e., food, medicine, as these were not unique to the Virginians, they were shared by the entire army. These aspects of the military of the Revolution are covered in many general histories of the conflict.

The reasons for choosing Virginians are:

1. The Continental Army was made up of units (regiments/battalions) provided by the individual states. The state was responsible (it did not always meet this responsibility) for the equipment used by its soldiers. This made each state's troops unique. Although any state's troops would have served the purpose of this study, the Virginia troops are used, as stated earlier, because Virginia was a leader in the Revolution and the attitudes of this regional society contributed to the beginnings of a national character during and after the war.

2. Infantry equipment was chosen, as the infantry represents the largest service arm of the Continental Army and, therefore, best represents the population as a whole. The other branches, cavalry and artillery, were, by comparison, specialized units that were a small part (numerically) of the total army. The material culture associated with these soldiers might not be representative due to the specific and limited function of these units. Also, these units, considered prestigious in the military of the period, tended to be led by individuals from the upper classes, although this was also true to some degree in the infantry.

3. Although Virginia organized and supported militia and regular units for service within the state, the units serving with the Continental Army had the opportunity to mix with units from other states. This opportunity was unusual in a country where geographic isolation was common. The Virginians of the Continental Army were part of a shared experience with men from other regions. Probably, from this experience, many

veterans had developed at least the seeds of a nationalistic mindset. This may have been less true among their fellow citizens who stayed at home.

The documentary evidence of equipment used by the Virginia soldier is not overwhelming in amount or detail. What is available provides a general impression of the clothing, arms and other items. The quality and quantity of this evidence vary through the eight years of the war. The periods of late 1775-early 1776 and late 1778-early 1779, are comparatively rich in records. The interim period is sketchy, at best. The final years of the war, 1780-1783, have little substantive information.

The equipment issued by the state to the soldiers early in the war is documented in the records of the Williamsburg Public Store. These records were transcribed and annotated in "Clothing and Accoutrements of the Officers and Soldiers of the Virginia Forces 1775-1780," by Mary Goodwin in 1962 (unpublished manuscript). Although they cover nearly six years of the war, the Williamsburg records are of the greatest value in understanding the initial supply of the soldiers mustering at Williamsburg in the autumn 1775-spring 1777. The records from the later years provide little information concerning supply to specific units.

What is noted in the later years of the Williamsburg records is the shipping of equipment north, much of it destined for distribution in Philadelphia. "Records of the Public Store, Philadelphia," detail the equipment distribution to the Virginia regiments during the autumn, winter and spring of 1778-1779. The large amount and variety of items issued in this period not only suggests the appearance of the Virginia regiments after this supply, but because of the necessity of this supply, speaks to the need of these troops before the issue.

The period between the initial equipment issue in Williamsburg and the Philadelphia "issue" is covered by deserter descriptions that appear as advertisements in two newspapers, the *Virginia Gazette* and *Pennsylvania Packet*. These descriptions suggest variety rather than uniformity in the Virginia line. Although the descriptions are of value, the small sample severely limits their value as a picture of the soldier's equipment.

Other primary sources available to this study are the collected writings of military and civilian leaders such as George Washington, Thomas Jefferson, George Weeden, Robert Gamble and Nathanael Greene. These sources contain correspondence and army orders that refer to equipment need, supply and quality of the equipment in use. That equipment was supplied is often inferred from the lack of further requests. These sources were essential in identifying the type of musket used by the Virginia soldier.

After determining what equipment was used by the soldiers, another group of sources was consulted to illustrate the military material culture of the American Revolution. These works, many published for the bicentennial of the war, are used by the collector of military equipment to identify and authenticate items. These sources rarely provide information concerning the history of a specific piece of equipment. Nor do they provide a large number of items to study. Usually, however, the samples typify the particular item.

Another source of information, or perhaps bias, that must be noted is the author's use of reproductions of the equipment being discussed. Two decades of participation in living history programs using reproductions of colonial period artifacts has provided unique insights concerning these items. An attempt has been made not to include speculative ideas and thoughts gained from this experience, as this activity has been approached as a hobby rather than experimental history, although there is a potential for research and questions have been pursued. Consequently, there is a possibility that this study has been influenced by these experiences.

There is included a very short essay on the service of the Virginia Continental Line. This chapter highlights the role the Virginians played in major engagements of the war and other contributions. This essay will not provide anything approaching a comprehensive view of the conflict. The reader is encouraged to seek a general history of the war. Page Smith's *A New Age Now Begins* is recommended.

The conclusion of this work will present some thoughts that developed from the original thesis but will not repeat the argument.

A BRIEF HISTORY OF THE VIRGINIANS
IN THE CONTINENTAL ARMY

Virginians served in the Continental Army throughout the American Revolution. At the beginning of the war, Daniel Morgan led his independent company of Virginia riflemen north to join the New Englanders besieging the British in Boston. They were part of that collection of citizen soldiers the Continental Congress adopted as the Continental Army. Although Morgan's company represented a small contribution in quantity, it displayed the colony's attitude and commitment to the conflict. From the outset, Virginia was ready to contribute to the war effort.

The delay of Virginia's regular regiments in joining the new Continental Army was due primarily to the lack of equipment and the confusion of forming a new military organization. When they did march north late in the summer of 1776, Virginians became a major part of Washington's army. Their importance to the main army continued until they were sent to defend Charleston, South Carolina, in 1780. In the closing years of the war, 1780-1783, Virginia's manpower contributions were limited to the Southern Department. Although most of the veteran Virginia Continental Line surrendered in 1780 with the garrison of Charleston, the state managed to raise additional men for service during the remainder of the war.

The response in Virginia began, as all threats of a hostile nature were handled at this time, by the militia being called to service. This new threat was not, however, the small bands of French and Indian raiders that menaced the frontier in the 1750's. The new opponent, the British Army, presented a challenge beyond the ability of the independent county-based militia. Similarly, it called for a larger regular establishment than the two provincial regiments raised in the French and Indian War. As it became apparent that the conflict was going to become general in nature, Virginia took aggressive action to institute a military establishment appropriate to the British threat. First, in July 1775, the state was divided into sixteen districts; each was to raise a battalion. Also, regular regiments were being formed. Between July and December of 1775, nine regiments of infantry were authorized by the government. Two regiments were completed by November, five were ready by February 1776, and two more were ready in the spring of that year.

Threats within the state by the Royal Governor, Lord Dunmore, and a separate British expedition against Charleston, South Carolina, to which the 8th Virginia responded, delayed the line regiments who were to march north to join Washington's Continental Army (Sellers 1978:2, 3-5). Virginia's Royal Governor, John Murray, Earl of Dunmore, when convinced the rebellion was a threat, rallied Virginia's loyalists and, from a base in Norfolk, raided along the tidewater rivers. He also called for the slaves to rise, promising them their freedom. Although the threat of a slave revolt, a constant concern in slave-holding areas, motivated the white Virginians opposing Dunmore and the King, it was far less effective among the slaves. Very few answered the call. The threat was sufficient, however, to send one of Virginia's new regiments of regulars to deal with Dunmore.

Two regiments were available: the 1st State Regiment, under the command of Patrick Henry, and the 2nd State Regiment under William Woodford. The troop returns of December 1775, shows the 2nd to be the larger of the two units (Lesser 1976:13). This, and the fact that Colonel Henry (although perhaps an inspirational leader) had no military experience, may have been the reason Woodford, a militia captain during the French and Indian War, received the assignment.

The swamps and rivers of tidewater Virginia dictated troop movements for both sides in this small campaign. Woodford's force, delayed in crossing the James River, moved slowly toward Norfolk. After an advanced party of Virginia militia was routed by British regulars who had come from Florida at Dunmore's call, the royal governor decided to block the Americans' march on Norfolk by fortifying his position at

Great Bridge (Chesapeake, Virginia). There he waited for Woodford's men.

The British blocked the road by building Fort Murray on the north side of the Elizabeth River. The river and swamps limited the approach to this fort to a single causeway and bridge. The Americans did not accept the invitation to conduct a suicidal assault on the fort. Instead, they built earthen fortifications at the south end of the causeway, fortified a church behind this forward position, and waited.

For a few weeks in late November and early December the two sides fought inconclusive small unit actions. On December 9, the British decided to force the issue and did what Woodford refused to do, assault fortifications along a narrow front. British grenadiers, elite soldiers, led the attack on the American works followed by other redcoat regulars, American loyalists, and the few who that had joined Dunmore. The slave battalion was known as the Royal Ethiopians. There were approximately 230 men in the attacking force.

The American front line was manned by ninety soldiers under the command of Lieutenant Edward Travis. Travis' men waited until the British were in effective range of their muskets and then fired a volley that stopped the attack. The loyalists lost heart and ran away, but the British regulars reformed and brought artillery into play. At the same time, Woodford was attempting to bring relief to the front.

The British cannon fired on the American works and their infantry renewed the assault. Believing that the artillery fire had driven the Americans away, the British pressed on only to find the Virginians, who had been under cover, rising to fire a devastating volley into the Redcoats at short range. The British attack was decisively stopped. Now the Americans followed with a counterattack, driving the enemy back and forcing Dunmore to abandon his fortifications and retreat through Norfolk to ships offshore.

The Virginians occupied Norfolk and were soon joined by troops from North Carolina led by Colonel Robert Howe. Howe assumed total command of the American forces that now comprised his own 2nd North Carolina, the 1st and 2nd Virginia State Regiments, the Culpepper Minute Battalion and

GREAT BRIDGE

December 1775

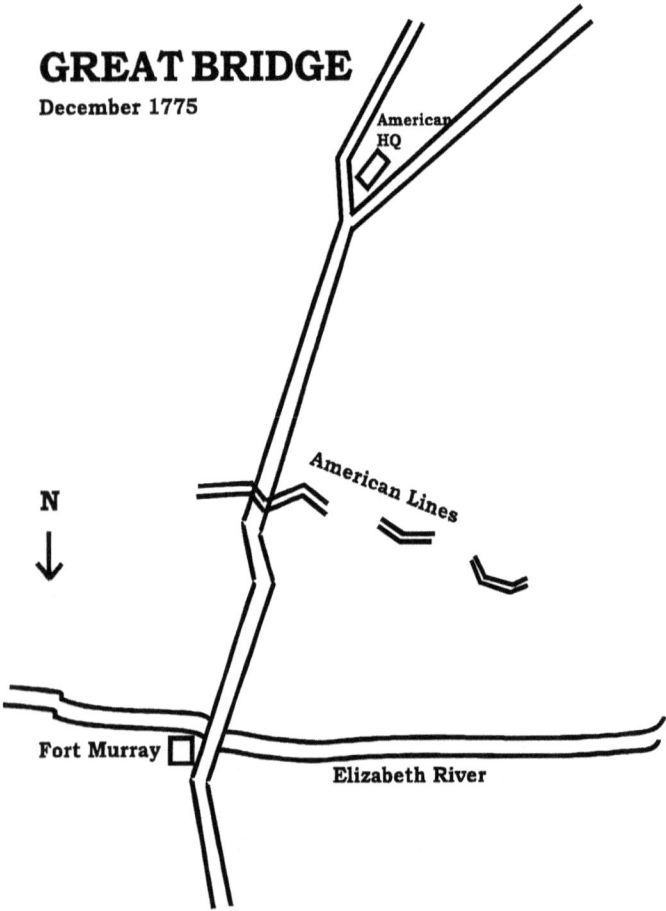

American
HQ

American Lines

N

↓

Fort Murray

Elizabeth River

the Southern Minute Battalion: a total of 1364 men. Dunmore stayed on his ships and at one point even requested supplies from Howe. When his request was refused, he bombarded the town and sent a party ashore to burn what round shot missed. Then he sailed away. Norfolk was destroyed, providing a strong propaganda device for the American cause (Smith I, 1976:622-624. Marshall and Peckham 1976:10-11. Lesser 1976:13).

Further south the British attempted their first large-scale offensive movement of the war. They were convinced that American loyalist sentiment was strongest in the southern colonies and, in the summer of 1776, sent a strong force to take Charleston, South Carolina, and its fine harbor as a base for further operations. The Americans countered this move by fortifying strategic islands in the seaward approaches to the city. This action blocked passage of shipping in the harbor. Although a British troop landing was made on an island that had not been occupied by the Americans, it was futile, as were the naval bombardments of the American forts. Unable to get into range where they could bombard the town, the British sailed away.

Virginia contributed the newly raised 8th Regiment, commanded by Peter Muhlenberg, to the Charleston garrison of 3761 men. The 535 soldiers of the 8th represent the largest regiment in Charleston. The march south and/or the South Carolina weather may have taken its toll as 150 men of the 8th are listed as sick in July 1776, many more than any other regiment in this garrison (Marshall and Peckham 1976:16-17. Lesser 1976:27).

With this initial threat to the South eliminated, the focus of the war moved north. By the late summer of 1776, the British, who had been driven from Boston, had regrouped in Halifax, Nova Scotia, and descended upon New York City with determination. The Virginians arrived for service with Washington's Continental Army just in time to take part in the defense of the city. The English, with the dominance of their navy, attacked New York City from the sea. The waterways in this area were the key to the city's defense and the Americans could muster no opposition to the English fleet. Beginning with the Battle of Long Island, Washington's army fought a series of defensive engagements. Washington undoubtedly understood the tactical problems he faced, however, the wavering morale of his army and the rebellion demanded an effort to defend America's largest city.

The British flanked the American position on Long Island causing Washington to fall back to Manhattan. The British continued to out-maneuver the Americans by land and especially by water, where they had no power, and pushed them up the island. The Americans rallied at a fortified position on Harlem Heights. The 3rd Virginia Regiment arrived in time to take a position in the fortifications on Harlem Heights. The Americans constructed three parallel lines of defense, each manned by a division of the army. On September 16, as his troops continued to strengthen this position, Washington sent Lieutenant Colonel (Captain in some sources) Thomas Knowlton with 150 of his Connecticut Rangers forward to scout the British. This reconnaissance began a small, but important battle in which Virginia's regulars saw their first action with the Continental Army.

Knowlton and his men came upon two battalions of British light infantry. The English attacked and the rangers took cover behind a stone wall and fired. They were persevering against the "lights" when part of the 42nd Regiment (the Black Watch) appeared on their left flank. This threat caused Knowlton to order a retreat that was accomplished with order.

The British light infantry followed but halted out of range of the main American position. Washington had heard the firing from Knowlton's party and sent Colonel Joseph Reed to investigate. Reed reported the situation and proposed a counterattack that he volunteered to lead. Washington agreed with Reed and one regiment was ordered to feint at the British front, while Knowlton's men, reinforced by three companies of Virginia riflemen from George Weedon's 3rd Regiment, conducted a flanking movement designed to take the British from the rear. Major Andrew Leitch commanded the Virginians.

The advance on the front was led by Lieutenant Colonel Archibald Crary with 150 men. They began a firefight with the

British and then gave way to bring the enemy deeper into the trap. Washington added to the deception by sending John Nixon's brigade forward to support Crary. This action continued for an hour while the flanking party, guided by Colonel Reed, made their way unnoticed around the British flank. Due to a lack of discipline, not surprising with inexperienced troops, the flanking party attacked the British from the side rather than from the rear. The British seized the opening and gave way, rapidly retreating across an open field until they could safely reform. Crary pushed them from one side and Reed from another. Knowlton and Leitch had been mortally wounded. The Americans, having been chased for a month, had now seen the backs of their enemy, and were inspired by their success.

Washington was no less animated by this success. He sent forward nine companies of Marylanders, Sargent's Brigade (Connecticut and Massachusetts), and the rest of Weedon's 3rd Virginia. American artillery moved forward and, with its fire added to that of the American infantry, the British were again forced to retreat. This brought additional English light troops and more Black Watch into the fray. As the American reinforcements arrived, the British commander was forced to commit his reserves, Grenadiers, the 33rd Regiment, a battalion of Hessians, a company of jaegers (German riflemen), and artillery. The retreating enemy met their advancing relief. The British now numbered about five thousand.

Washington, wisely, did not want to take the gamble of starting a general battle. To lose the battle meant to lose the revolution. He ordered the troops to retire. The men returned to their lines with a new spirit. Southerners had fought alongside New Englanders and had beaten the British. What is more important, the British commander, General Howe, who at this moment could have probably crushed Washington's army, if not the rebellion, went on the defensive for four weeks. This was an important interlude. It allowed Washington to plan, the army to rest, and it brought winter, the end of the campaign season, a month closer (Smith I, 1976:769-772. Ward I, 1952:247-252).

The 1st Virginia Regiment joined the army as it left New York and marched into New Jersey. On November 23, 1776, the 4th, 5th, and 6th Virginia Regiments joined the army at New Brunswick, New Jersey, forming a brigade of 745 men under Adam Stephen (Sellers 1978:6-7,9,11. Lesser 1976:40). The other Virginia Regiments, brigaded under the command of General George Weedon, mustered only 683 men (Lesser 1976:37). These two understrength brigades, totaling 1428 men, represented one-third of Washington's army.

This was the low point of the war for the Americans. Although the success of Harlem Heights had worn away with the memory of other defeats in the summer's campaign, having to give up New York was devastating. Washington was under pressure to revive morale and to use his army before short-term enlistments ran out on January 1. This resulted in his attack on the Hessian post at Trenton, New Jersey, on the day after Christmas, 1776. The army returns dated December 22, 1776, show that the army had 6104 men fit for duty. Virginians in this figure amounted to 915. The returns also list 764 Virginians as sick, 692 of these men from the 1st and 3rd Virginia of Weedon's brigade (Lesser 1976:43).

The Virginians were among the first to cross the Delaware River and advance on Trenton. Stephen's Brigade, the 4th, 5th, and 6th Virginia, was given the task of securing the landing on the New Jersey shore. Adam Stephen had served as the lieutenant colonel of Washington's Virginia Regiment during the French and Indian War. Although he had never shown himself to be a creative officer, he was a fighter. This probably was the reason for his assignment. The crossing accomplished, his brigade then led General Nathanael Greene's column toward Trenton on the Pennington road. This force included the other Virginia troops under William Stirling's command (Ward 1952:294).

Washington's plan was to attack Trenton simultaneously from the north and south. General John Sullivan, leading New England and New York troops, marched by the River Road and passed the town on the west. Then they took a position in front of the bridge over Assunpink Creek and faced north.

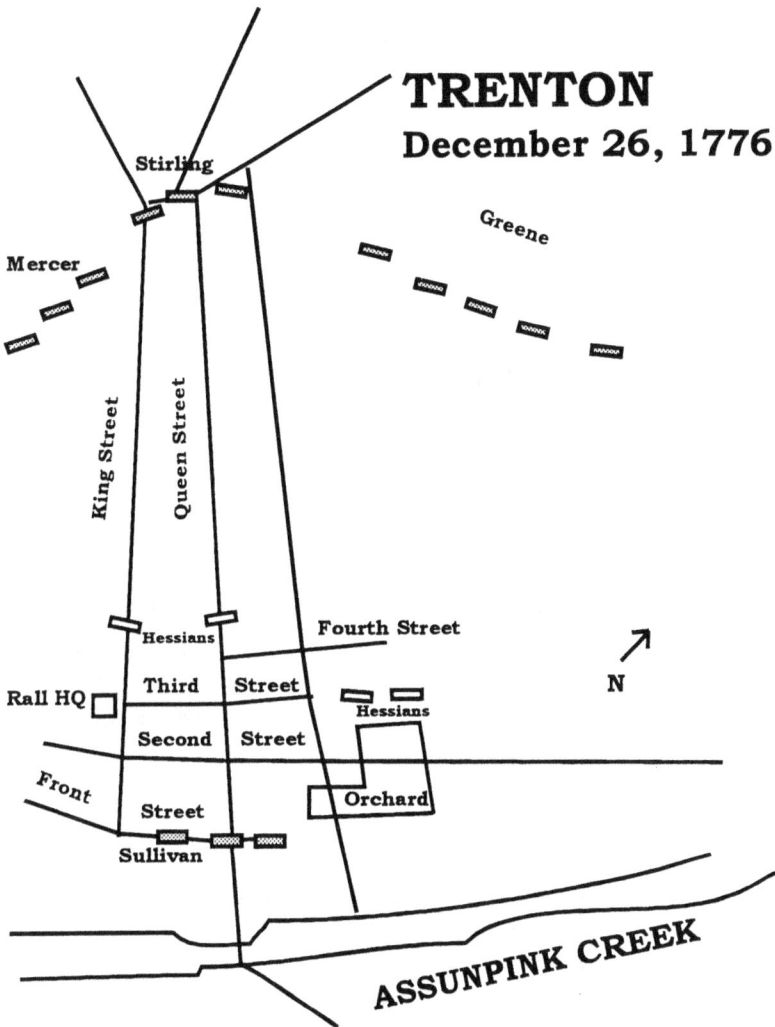

TRENTON

December 26, 1776

Stirling

Greene

Mercer

King Street

Queen Street

Fourth Street

Hessians

N

Rall HQ

Third Street

Hessians

Second Street

Front

Orchard

Street

Sullivan

ASSUNPINK CREEK

Washington had Greene's command form on the north side of town at the head of King Street and Queen Street. These two streets ran parallel and were the main north-south arteries through Trenton.

Stephen's Virginians, the advance guard, moved to the left, taking a position northeast of the town. Mercer's men took the other flank and formed a line between the town and the river. Stirling deployed his troops at the head of the streets, putting Weedon's Virginians on King Street. They were supported by artillery firing on the Hessians who, now alarmed, attempted to form in defense of the town. The enemy tried to bring their artillery into action but the American fire eliminated this threat. They then attempted an infantry advance on the American position but the artillery punished them severely. This was followed by an American bayonet charge down both streets. The Virginians, led by Captain William Washington and Lieutenant James Monroe, captured a Hessian artillery battery. Both officers were wounded in this action.

The battle developed into several small actions, this due to the buildings that limited the maneuvers of larger formations. German units would break and attempt to regroup only to find a new threat from a different direction. The Hessian commander, Colonel Rall, mortally wounded, ordered his men to rally at the orchard to the southeast of the town. This was met by fire from Stephen's Virginians. The Hessians began to surrender. Nine hundred forty-eight men became prisoners. There were twenty-two Hessian dead and ninety-two wounded. American losses amounted to four wounded. It is estimated that five hundred of the enemy escaped.

The attack on Trenton and the raid on Princeton that followed, although small actions in terms of numbers of troops, were important. The morale problem that led to these offensive actions by Washington was solved, at least for the moment. The victory at Trenton gave the Americans a success in tactical maneuver against professional European soldiers. Also, it may have greatly influenced France and other countries to support and provide aid to the Americans.

In January 1777, the 2nd and 7th Regiments were ordered to march north and join their fellow Virginians with

Washington. They experienced delays due to sickness and reached the Continental Army in April. The 8th Virginia arrived in late March. The 13th Virginia had been ordered to join the main army, but was then assigned to the frontier garrison of Fort Pitt (Pittsburgh, Pennsylvania). Returns show that the 10th, 11th, and 12th Regiments were also with the army in April (Sellers 1978:22-24. Lesser 1976:45).

The campaign of 1777 was a turning point in the war. Washington's forces did not have the numbers or the ability to conduct an offensive campaign and therefore had to follow the British lead. The British plan was to divide the New England states from the rest of the colonies by capturing the Hudson River-Lake Champlain line from Canada to New York City. An army, under General John Burgoyne, was to move south from Canada and eventually link with the main British force, commanded by William Howe, moving north from New York City.

The Americans thought that the British also had designs on capturing Philadelphia, the meeting place of the Continental Congress. Washington was forced to deal with both possibilities. The Northern Department was reinforced. Under the command of Horatio Gates, by the time of the climactic battle of Saratoga, it had the responsibility of stopping Burgoyne. Washington positioned himself to protect Philadelphia, but also to be able to move north if required.

There are no army records of troop strength for June through September 1777. The May return of the Continental Army lists twelve Virginia Line regiments (1st-12th) totaling 2512 men fit for duty. The Virginia contingent represented more than a third of Washington's force of 7363 infantry (Lesser 1976:46).

The threat to Philadelphia held Washington in Pennsylvania. The Northern Army had to deal with Burgoyne on their own. In a series of battles collectively called Saratoga (New York), they stopped the British move south, defeated the Redcoats in European style battles, and Burgoyne was compelled to surrender to Gates. In this campaign a corps of riflemen, commanded by Virginian Daniel Morgan, played an important role. Not only were they part of the final battle that

sealed the fate of Burgoyne's army, but legend says that
Morgan, with regret, ordered his riflemen to kill British
General Fraser who was attempting to rally the English and
German troops.

Part of the reason for Burgoyne's failure was that William
Howe did not support him. The British army in New York City
moved against Philadelphia by sailing to the head of
Chesapeake Bay. Washington positioned his army along
Brandywine Creek at Chadd's Ford, blocking the British line of
march from their landing site to Philadelphia.

The Battle of Brandywine was fought on September 11,
1777. The British began the action by demonstrating against the
American center at Chadd's Ford, while Lord Cornwallis led
half the British army north to cross the stream above the
American right flank. The Americans were taken by surprise.
When this end-run was finally discovered, the American right
flank attempted to pivot from their north-south alignment and
to reform east-west to face Cornwallis' British. They were only
partially successful. Adam Stephen's Virginians, along with the
Maryland brigade of Prudhomme de Borre and Stirling's
division formed on high ground. General John Sullivan, the
commander of the American right flank, and the rest of his
troops hurried to support Stephen, de Borre, and Stirling. He
arrived late and in the confusion failed to connect with the left
side of the new American line.

The Americans had a strong position and the British were
tired. They had been on the march since before daylight, it was
now mid-afternoon. Nevertheless, the English and Germans
came on with determination. De Borre's brigade broke and ran.
Stephen realigned his troops to cover the gap on his right and
his men and Stirling's held. Sullivan personally joined this
group but the men he had brought forward were attacked and
routed before they could form a line. The Americans,
outnumbered and in danger of being flanked, held this
position for about an hour and forty-five minutes.

Washington understood the new situation and realigned his
remaining troops at Chadd's Ford. He ordered Anthony
Wayne's and William Maxwell's brigades with Proctor's
artillery to hold the ford and he formed a reserve, under

Brandywine

September 11, 1777

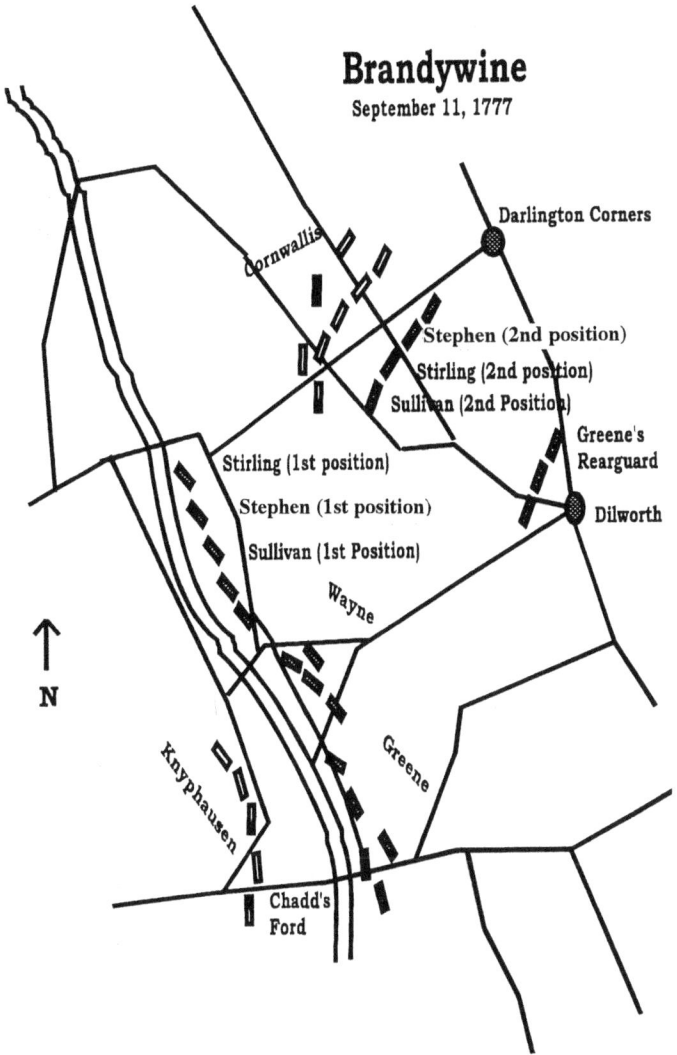

Darlington Corners

Cornwallis

Stephen (2nd position)

Stirling (2nd position)

Sullivan (2nd Position)

Greene's
Rearguard

Stirling (1st position)

Stephen (1st position)

Sullivan (1st Position)

Dilworth

Wayne

N

Greene

Knyphausen

Chadd's
Ford

Nathanael Greene, of Weedon's and Muhlenberg's Virginians, including the inexperienced 13th and 14th Virginia. These regiments, along with the 15th Virginia, had apparently joined the army after the May return was recorded. Washington was fighting on two fronts and both were outnumbered. He committed his reserves to support Sullivan on the right.

General Greene moved his command five miles in forty-five minutes and established a line in the face of Sullivan's retreating troops. These regiments, seeing their first action, held the British force for forty-five minutes as Sullivan's men retreated. Sunset allowed Greene's men to execute an orderly withdrawal. Losses for the British were less than six hundred. The American loses are not known but were probably near one thousand. (Ward I,1952:352-354).

Washington had avoided a decisive defeat, but for the British the way to Philadelphia was now open. Washington reorganized, followed the British and attacked them at Germantown on October 4th. The American plan was to attack in four columns. Greene, still commanding the Virginians who had fought so well at Brandywine, was positioned on the American left and was ordered to flank the British right. Greene's command had a long distance to march on a foggy morning and they were misled by their guide. This was only one of many problems that plagued the Americans that day. Consequently, the timing of the operation was thrown off.

The attack in the center was initially successful, although the main American force became stalled when the English fortified in the Chew House, its brick walls strong enough to withstand light artillery fire. Not wanting to leave a fortified position in his rear, Washington stalled his attack. This decided the battle as Greene's command, not sure of their location, heard the firing and, without orders, Stephen moved his brigade toward the sound of the guns. He probably thought that the main column had engaged the body of the enemy. Unexpectedly, and through a mist, he came upon Anthony Wayne's men and the two American forces fired on each other.

Greene, with the rest of his division, met an advancing British force at Luken's Mill. There was hard fighting but the British finally gave way. Greene readjusted his line to the right

Main American Force

Greene's Force

Chew House

Meeting House

Luken's Mill

N

Market House

British Camp

Howe's HQ

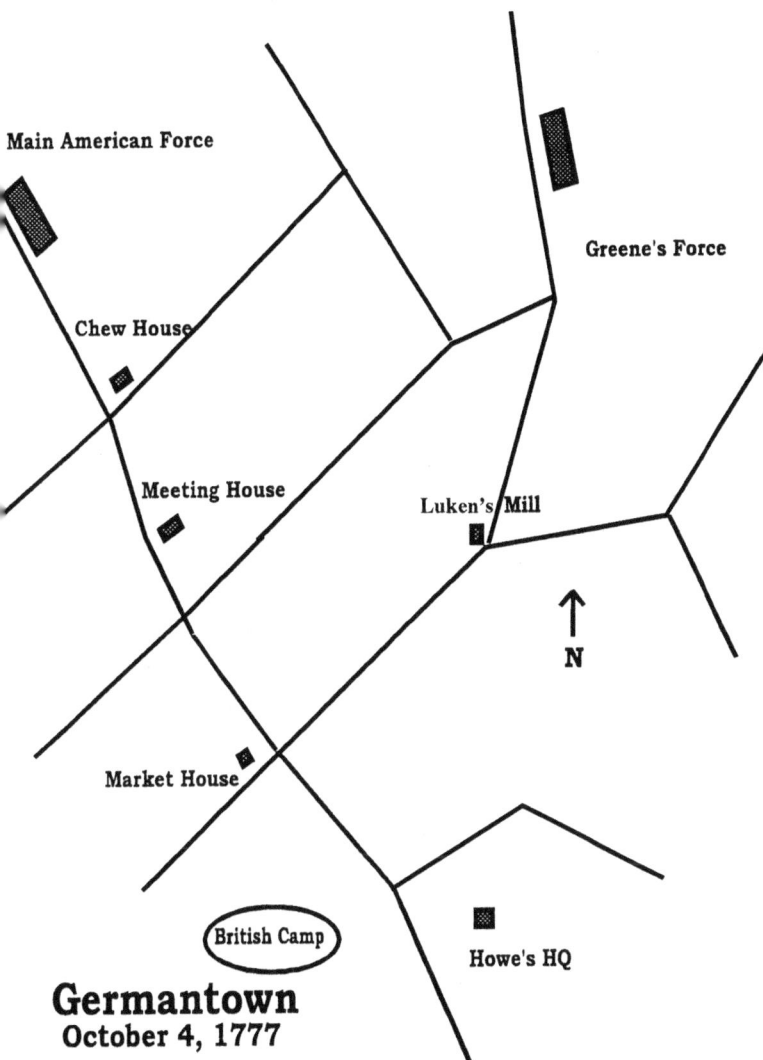

Germantown
October 4, 1777

and attacked the market house. Muhlenberg led a bayonet charge that penetrated the British position and his men momentarily entered the enemy camp.

The other American columns, held up by the British advanced guard, had used most of their ammunition and started to withdraw. This allowed the British to concentrate on Greene. He now faced the enemy on two sides. Muhlenberg led another bayonet charge to escape being surrounded. Greene's entire command, tired from a night march and a battle, was now forced to conduct a fighting retreat. The Virginians' losses, including killed, wounded, and missing were 348. The army's total loss was more than 1173. Not recorded in these figures is that General Adam Stephen was found intoxicated and was forced to leave the army (Ward I, 1952:363-371. Sellers 1978:39).

Washington, to maintain a watch on the British, established the army's winter quarters at Valley Forge. Enlistments in the Virginia regiments were expiring and the state was having trouble meeting its quota. The number of companies in each regiment was reduced from ten to eight. This allowed the extra officers to leave the army for recruiting duty but did not make up for the manpower shortage. The state had no alternative but to send the 1st and 2nd State Line Regiments to serve with the Continental Army (Sellers 1978:43). The service of the State Line Regiments was intended to be within the borders of Virginia.

The British left Philadelphia and returned to New York City in the spring and summer of 1778. An attack on the British rearguard resulted in the indecisive Battle of Monmouth, the last major engagement of the war in the middle and northern states. The Continental Army, under Washington, would now sit and wait until it moved south to Yorktown, Virginia, in the autumn of 1781.

The manpower problems of the Virginia Line continued. In September 1778, the Virginia Line was reorganized by consolidation of understrength units and the renumbering of regiments. The fifteen regiments were reduced to eleven (Sellers 1978:49). This allowed many officers to begin recruiting activity. The October 1778, return shows the Virginia

Continental Line, including the 1st and 2nd State Line Regiments, had 3594 men, however, only 2376 were present and fit for duty. This represents 216 men per regiment, less than half the ideal strength. This situation would get worse (Lesser 1976:88-89). The recruiting effort included increased bonuses. Apparently, it was successful. Officers and men available for duty increased from 1090 in February 1779, to 2281 in August. This increase is perhaps not entirely attributable to new enlistments but may include sick men returning to duty (Lesser 1976:104, 128).

There were two small actions in 1779. "Mad" Anthony Wayne, commanding the Corps of Light Infantry, captured the British post at Stony Point, New York, and a force under "Light Horse Harry" Lee raided a post at Paulus Hook, New Jersey. Virginia troops were involved in these actions. After capture, both posts were abandoned by the Americans and then reoccupied by the British, so the activity seems to have had no strategic value and was probably a result of the aggressive personalities of the commanders. The year ended with the Virginia Line being ordered south to counter another British attempt to separate the southern states. Again, the British acted on their belief that the South had strong loyalist sentiment.

The final return of Virginia Line serving under Washington is in January 1780. It reflects a combination of units that first appear in the returns of the Southern Department in April 1780. Before joining the garrison defending Charleston, South Carolina, the 1st, 10th, 5th, 11th, and 7th Regiments had become the 1st Virginia Regiment. The 2nd, 3rd, and 4th Regiments had become the 2nd Virginia Regiment. The 6th and 8th Regiments, and an independent command under Nathanael Gist, became the 3rd Virginia Regiment. There were, in addition, three Virginia Detachments recruited in 1779. The 1st and 2nd Detachments went to Charleston. The 3rd was slow in raising men and finding equipment and missed the British siege of the city. (Lesser 1976:148, 160).

Charleston surrendered on May 12, 1780, with over 700 Virginians among the garrison of five thousand (Sellers 1978:62, 67). The remaining Virginia unit, the 3rd Detachment, finally marched south and on May 29 was caught near

Waxhaws, South Carolina, by British forces and overwhelmed. All that remained of the Virginia Line were the 226 men of the 9th Regiment (former 13th Virginia), part of the garrison of Fort Pitt and other posts on the Pennsylvania-Virginia frontier. (Lesser 1976:169).

Virginia attempted to reconstitute the Line by raising seven new regiments recruited for 18 months. However, by the time of the Battle of Camden, August 16, 1780, not one regiment had been completed. The state did send fourteen hundred militia to the Southern Department (Sellers 1978:62, 67, 69, 70-71). These men were on the American left at Camden. The British attacked the American right. The Virginians moved slowly and cautiously to support the troops being attacked but they were late. Apparently, the Virginians believed all was lost and they broke and ran.

Virginia did raise regular regiments for the Southern Department by February 1781. Returns show 548 men in the Virginia Continental Brigade along with 727 militia under Edward Stevens (Lesser 1976:196). This officer commanded 750 militia at Yorktown later that year. Also at Yorktown was Robert Lawson in command of 750 Virginia militia (Kemp 1776:45). He, like Stevens, had seen action in the Southern Department. They took part in the Battle at Guilford Courthouse that eventually led to Cornwallis' retreat to Yorktown. It seems reasonable to speculate that the militiamen under their command at Yorktown had seen action in Greene's campaign against Cornwallis.

Guilford Courthouse was the finale of a classic campaign between two of the war's best commanders, Charles Cornwallis and Nathanael Greene. Greene was appointed to the Southern Department after Horatio Gates had lost the Battle of Camden (South Carolina), August 16, 1780. He joined what was left of Gates' army on December 2 at Charlotte, North Carolina, assuming command on the following day.

Cornwallis had thoughts of moving into Virginia to help the British activity begun by Benedict Arnold, now serving in a British uniform. If he left the Carolinas, however, he would only allow Greene to support the raids by partisans such as

Thomas Sumpter and Francis Marion, *The Swamp Fox*. Greene forced the issue by sending Daniel Morgan and six hundred men toward South Carolina. Cornwallis dispatched Colonel Banastre Tarleton with a small elite force after Morgan. He followed with the rest of his army.

Morgan turned on Tarleton at a clearing in the woods known as the Cowpens. The Americans formed three parallel lines. Riflemen made up the widely deployed first line. The second line was formed of militia and Morgan, realizing their questionable discipline, asked them to only fire a few rounds before falling back. His third line was posted on a slight rise and consisted of Marylanders and Virginians. The Maryland men were regulars and the Virginians have been identified as regulars and also as militia. The truth may be that they had been organized as militia but the ranks contained many Continental Army veterans. Despite their official designation, they performed like regulars during the battle. Behind this position Morgan placed William Washington's cavalry.

Tarleton had the reckless abandon of the cavalryman and the usual low opinion of the Americans, shared by most British commanders. He had pushed his soldiers hard to catch Morgan and immediately forced his tired men into line for an attack. His effort began by advancing some of his mounted troops to clear the woods of Morgan's first line. The American riflemen emptied many saddles, thus halting this maneuver. The British line now advanced and the riflemen fell back.

The second American line did all that was asked of them. They did some damage to the oncoming enemy and then broke for the rear. The apparent retreat of the Americans caused the British to come on faster chasing the retreating militia. The British line lost some of its regularity in the pursuit and Morgan sent Washington's cavalry to support the militia. Washington's appearance momentarily stopped the British and this allowed the militia to gather behind the American third line.

Tarleton reformed his effort and committed his entire infantry, including the Scots of the 71st Regiment, against the Americans. The Continental regulars in the third line held and sent an effective fire toward the enemy. The British extended their line beyond the right flank of the Americans. Countering this movement, the Virginians turned to the rear to swing the right of their line back to oppose the flanking attempt by the enemy. When the British noticed the Virginians maneuver, they assumed the Americans were retreating, and came on with abandon. Morgan, it is said, also thought the Virginians were retreating and rode to their position only to be informed, less than politely, of the purpose of the maneuver. The Virginians, reaching the desired position faced about and delivered a devastating volley into the oncoming British. Then, joined by the Marylanders, they charged the enemy. The militia, which had reformed, joined in and the British line broke. Tarleton was able to escape with some of his mounted men aggressively pursued by Washington's cavalry. The British lost 100 killed and 229 wounded. Thirty-nine British officers were killed. Perhaps this was due to several riflemen in Morgan's force, who saw officers as priority targets. The prisoners numbered 600. Morgan lost 12 killed and 60 wounded (Smith 1976:1457).

Morgan was correct in assuming that the main British force had to be closing in on him. He retreated toward Virginia with Cornwallis in pursuit. As Greene moved his force north to join Morgan, he was making plans to take a position on the north side of the Dan River. Cornwallis, knowing that he had to move quickly if he were to force a battle with Greene, burned his baggage, turning his whole force into a light corps. He was unable to overtake the Americans who, covered by Virginian cavalry, had finished crossing the Dan on February 13, leaving no boats on the south shore for the English. The chase had exhausted the English and Cornwallis retreated to Hillsboro, North Carolina.

Greene did not hesitate. He sent cavalry and light troops south. This was to keep loyalist sentiment from gaining strength due to his retreat. He recrossed the Dan on February 23. Fights between small units and strategic movements brought the armies together at Guilford Courthouse on March 15, 1781.

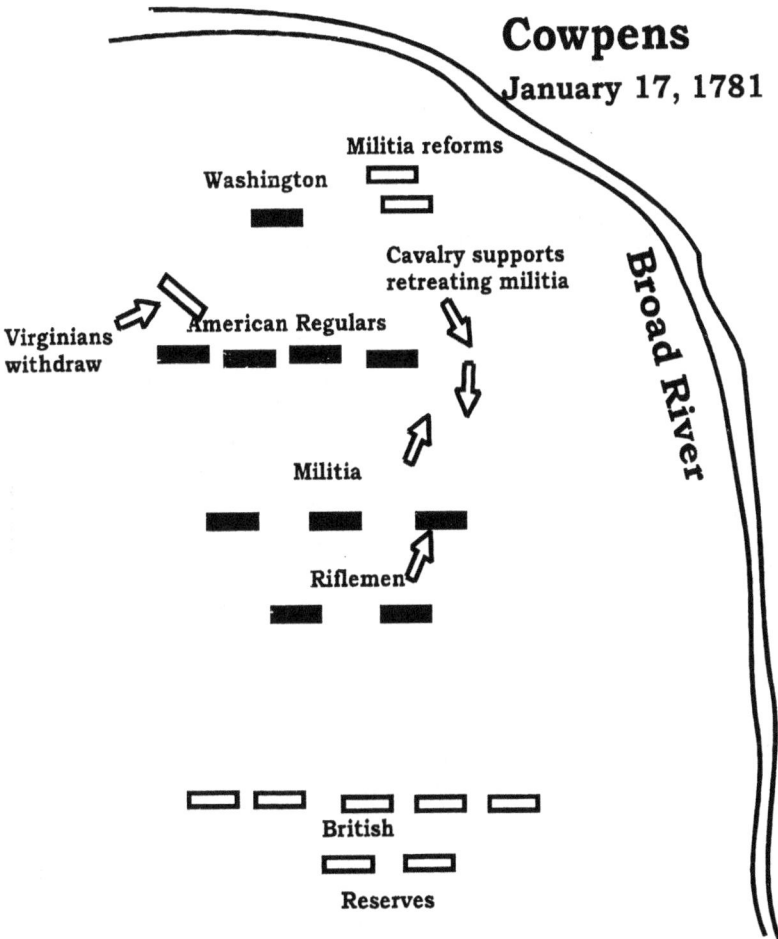

Cowpens
January 17, 1781

Militia reforms

Washington

Cavalry supports
retreating militia

Virginians
withdraw

American Regulars

Broad River

Militia

Riflemen

British

Reserves

Henry "Light-Horse Harry" Lee and his cavalry reported the advance of Cornwallis. Following Morgan's successful tactics at Cowpens, Greene formed his troops in three parallel lines. The first line was made up of North Carolina militia with artillery commanding the road on which the enemy was expected. The second line, on the wooded slope leading up to the courthouse, was held by Virginia militia under Stevens and Lawson. On the crest of the hill were Continental Regulars, two regiments of Marylanders on the left and two regiments of Virginians, under Christopher Greene and Samuel Hawes, on the right. A mixed force of infantry and cavalry secured the flanks, in line with the North Carolinians in front. William Washington's cavalry with a small contingent of Delaware regulars and Virginia riflemen was on the right. Lee's Legion, cavalry and infantry, with riflemen under William Campbell were on the left.

The British deployed upon coming in sight of the Americans. Four regiments made up their front, Cornwallis reserving his grenadiers, light infantry, two battalions of Guards, and the cavalry. They advanced across a clearing toward the North Carolina militia who were positioned behind a rail fence. The Carolinians fired a volley at extreme range and then broke. The American artillery, now without support, was forced to withdraw in the face of the oncoming enemy.

The English found stiffer opposition when they advanced into the woods and came upon the Virginia militia. Simultaneously they were being hurt by the American flanking parties. Cornwallis had to commit his reserves, except the cavalry, to break the second American line and deal with the riflemen on his flanks. With the American riflemen occupied and the Virginia militia in retreat, the English regulars advanced upon the Continentals.

The British left flank had a difficult time with the American right. They could not ignore the fire from Col. Charles Lynch's riflemen supported by Robert Kirkwood's Delaware regulars. The Americans fought tree to tree as they slowly pulled back. The British center, suffering many casualties, was stopped by the regulars of the 1st Maryland. Cornwallis sent the 1st Battalion of the Guards to help the attack in the center. They charged the inexperienced 2nd Maryland and the Marylanders ran. The 1st Maryland turned to save their comrades and William Washington's cavalry joined the melee. The British fell back. The 1st Maryland followed with the bayonet.

Cornwallis saved his command by ordering his artillery to fire into his retreating troops and the pursuing Americans. This stopped the Americans and allowed the British to escape. Both sides regrouped. Again, the British attacked the 1st Maryland and shifted to also engage Hawes' Virginians. The British were unable to make any gains. The fights on the flanks had gone badly for them. Probably both generals were unaware of the true situation. If they had been, Cornwallis would have retreated and Greene would not have started his withdrawal.

Christopher Greene's Virginians deployed to cover the withdrawal and the Americans marched away. The American casualties amounted to 227 with more than a thousand men missing, mostly North Carolina militia. The British had 554 killed and wounded, more than a quarter of Cornwallis' force. The British held the field but lost any remaining support from loyalists. Cornwallis rested his command and eventually marched to Yorktown. Greene headed south, deeper into the Carolinas.

The Yorktown returns show a 1223 man Virginia and Pennsylvania Brigade under the command of Anthony Wayne. Other sources suggest this brigade might have been smaller with Virginia contributing 350 men and Pennsylvania with two battalions of 275 men each (Lesser 1976:210. Kemp 1976:45). As mentioned before, two veterans of Greene's southern campaign, Edward Stevens and Robert Lawson, commanded militia brigades during the siege. George Weedon commanded a third brigade.

Two regiments of Virginia Continental regulars fought with Greene throughout the South capturing small British posts. With an army of about two thousand men, Greene moved through the Carolinas and fought his last major engagement of the war at Eutaw Springs on September 8, 1781. Greene had a core of experienced regulars supported by militia and tough southern partisan troops under leaders like Francis Marion.

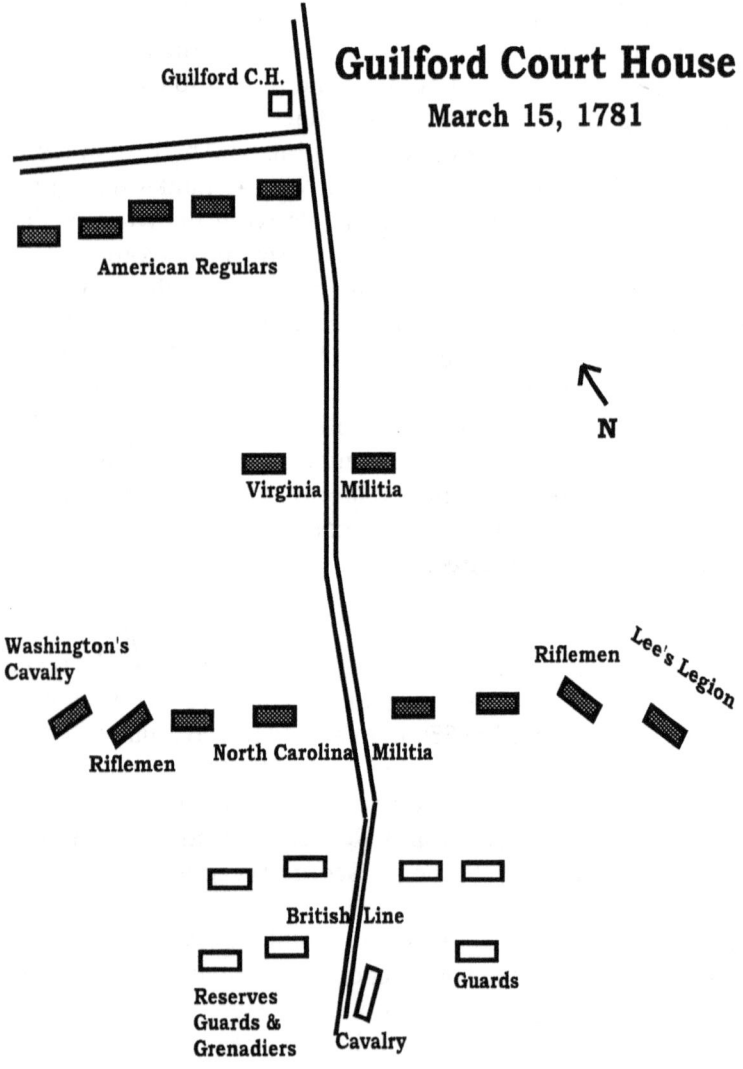

Guilford Court House

March 15, 1781

Guilford C.H.

American Regulars

N

Virginia Militia

Washington's Cavalry

Riflemen

Lee's Legion

Riflemen

North Carolina Militia

British Line

Guards

Reserves
Guards &
Grenadiers

Cavalry

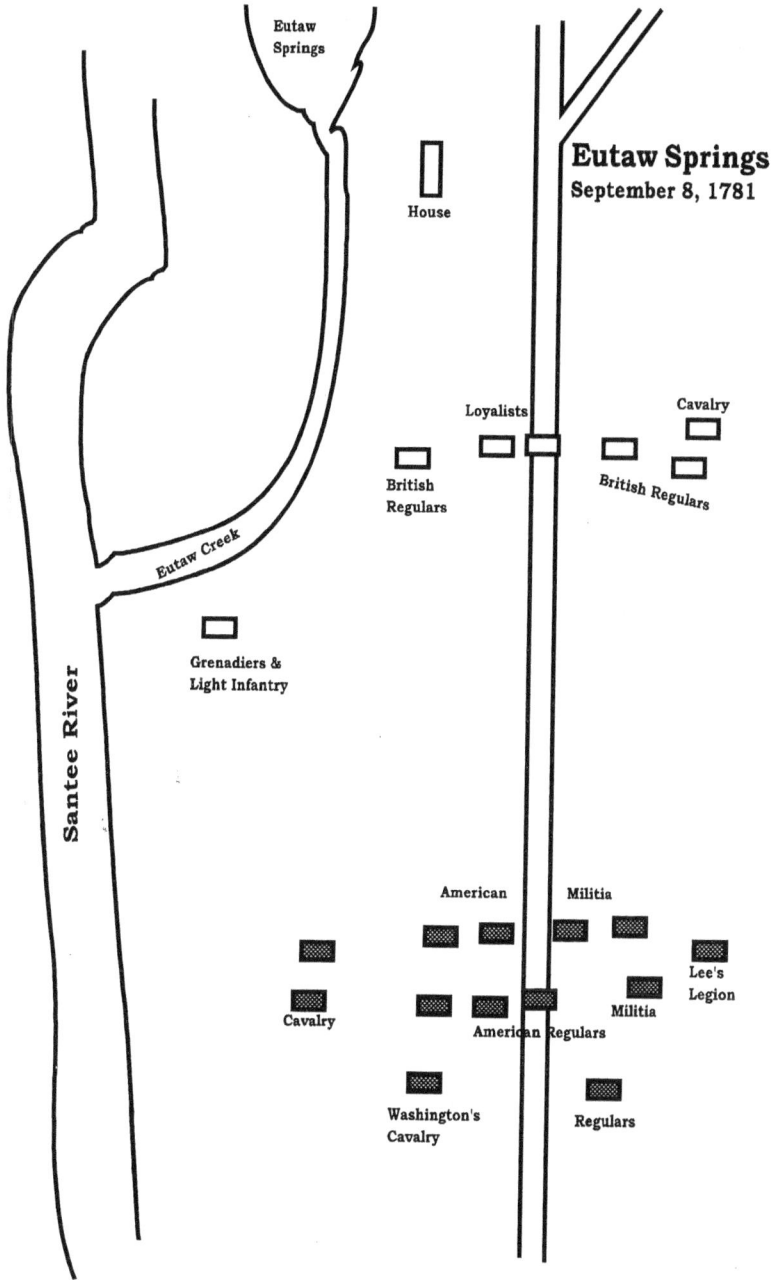

Eutaw
Springs

House

Eutaw Springs
September 8, 1781

Loyalists

Cavalry

British
Regulars

British Regulars

Eutaw Creek

Grenadiers &
Light Infantry

Santee River

American

Militia

Lee's
Legion

Cavalry

Militia

American Regulars

Washington's
Cavalry

Regulars

The British force was mostly regulars with some American loyalists. The Americans attacked with the militia in the lead. They did well until the British brought overwhelming force against them. As they broke, the British followed, only to be confronted by a second line of American regulars who attacked with the bayonet. Simultaneously, the American flanks were able to join the center and the British broke and retreated in disorder. They were pushed through their camp and would have been overwhelmed had not the Virginian and Maryland regulars stopped to loot the British camp. This disorganized Greene's command and the British were able to regain the field. Now, however, both sides were exhausted. Greene pulled back and the next day the British marched away (Ward II,1952:830-833).

With the surrender at Yorktown on October 19, regulars, including Virginians, were sent to Greene's command. Anthony Wayne surrounded Savannah and the British evacuated the city in July 1782. Half of Wayne's men were Virginians (Smith II, 1976:1748. Lesser 1976:221). A detachment of Virginians remained with the army until mid-March 1783 when the last Virginia soldiers were discharged (Sellers 1978:72-73, 75).

INTRODUCTION TO UNIFORMS AND EQUIPMENT

There are many surviving pieces of military equipment from the American Revolution. Unfortunately, very few of these artifacts have documentation linking it to an individual soldier, military unit, or state. Consequently, it was necessary to look at primary and secondary documentary materials to discover what equipment was used by Virginia's soldiers. With this data it is possible to present a representative illustration.

The documentary evidence of equipment used by the Virginia soldier is not overwhelming in amount or detail. What is available, however, provides a general impression of the clothing, arms, and other common items. The quality and quantity of this evidence vary through the eight years of the war. The periods of late 1775-early 1776, and late 1778-early 1779, are comparatively rich in records. Other periods are sketchy, at best. During the final years of the war, 1780-1783, probably because the war had come to Virginia's soil, there are only scraps of information.

The equipment issued to the soldiers early in the war is documented in the records of the Williamsburg Public Store. These records were transcribed and annotated in "Clothing and Accouterments of the Officers and Soldiers of the Virginia Forces 1775-1780," by Mary Goodwin in 1962 (unpublished manuscript). Although they cover nearly six years of the war, the Williamsburg records are of most value in understanding the initial supply of those soldiers mustering at Williamsburg in the autumn of 1775 through the spring of 1777. The later years covered by this source provides little information concerning supplies sent to specific units.

What is noted in the later years of the Williamsburg records is the shipping of equipment north, much of it probably destined for distribution in Philadelphia. "Records of the Public Store, Philadelphia," details the distribution of equipment to the Virginia regiments during the autumn, winter, and spring of 1778-1779. The large amount and variety of items issued in this period not only illustrates the appearance of the Virginia regiments, but also speaks indirectly to the need of these troops before the issue.

The few deserter descriptions in the *Virginia Gazette* and *Pennsylvania Packet* allow very little confidence in applying these descriptions to the appearance of the Virginia troops in the middle part of the war. The difference among the descriptions, and when compared to the data available concerning the early and late periods of the war, does suggest that supply problems existed and the equipment of the Virginia soldiers was not uniform.

Other primary sources important to this study are the collected writings of military and civilian leaders such as George Washington, Thomas Jefferson, George Weedon, Robert Gamble, and Nathanael Greene. This correspondence and army orders refer to equipment need, supply and quality. These sources were essential in deciding the type of musket used by the Virginia soldier, and also other items of equipment.

This study uses sources that illustrate the military material culture of the American Revolution. These sources rarely provide information concerning the history of a specific piece of equipment. Nor do they provide a sample sufficiently large to accommodate a quantitative study. Also, the equipment is that produced in an age that is, at best, at the dawn of industrialization. Nearly all of the material used by the Virginia soldier is the product of craftsmen and women, working in small shops or at home. The reader should understand that the illustrations always represent a sample.

EQUIPMENT OF THE VIRGINIA CONTINENTAL LINE

CLOTHING

After the American troops besieging the British redcoats in Boston were adopted, in 1775, by the Continental Congress as the Continental Army, the Congress set about developing a military system. To balance the contributions of the individual states, a quota was established by which each state would be obligated to furnish a certain number of regiments. Virginia was to provide fifteen regiments. The state met this goal by 1777, and when the number of men in these regiments fell to a point where reorganization was necessary, Virginia sent two state line regiments to augment the continental regulars.

Clothing and equipping the soldiers of the Virginia Continental Line was an immense problem for the state, financially and logistically. It equaled, or perhaps exceeded, the difficulties of recruiting the men needed to fill the fifteen regiments. Virginia, by the standards of the times, did a good job in supplying these men with the equipment they needed to do their job. Histories that repeat the "ragtag" description, although this was at times true, often fail to consider that lack of supply was common to most military forces in the eighteenth century, the difficulty of transportation usually being the problem.

The Virginians marched to join George Washington's Continental Army when the individual regiments had sufficient men and equipment. Their clothing and other equipment did not meet the ideal of an eighteenth-century European soldier. Instead of wool coats the Virginians began the war substituting linen hunting shirts or frocks. The individual Virginian's equipment would also depend on what was available when he received his "issue." Uniformity of the regiment, or at least the company, was desired, but if blue breeches were available the soldier received blue. The next man, perhaps from the same company, might be the first to get an issue out of the next bale and these breeches might be green.

A soldier's clothing would quickly wear out if he were actively campaigning. It is doubtful that a garment would survive more than six months of marching, fighting, and temporary camps. During this time, he probably wore the same uniform day and night. In the rare times of plenty, when wool regimental coats had been issued, the use of a rifle frock or hunting shirt for daily duties such as gathering wood or building fortification would give added life to the coat. Similarly, the use of overalls and gaiters would help preserve the breeches and stockings. Yet, these items were not always available and they too succumbed to hard and constant use.

As with his original issue of clothing, replacement items came from what stock was available. A soldier might be issued new breeches of wool, linen, or buckskin. If he had money he might buy his own clothing from a civilian tailor. His clothing may have worn out at a different rate than that of other men due to the quality of material and construction, the care taken by the individual to maintain his clothing, and the duty to which he was assigned. If the soldier and his comrades were all uniform at one point in time, more than likely six months later there would be a noticeable variety in the uniforms.

Other factors affected uniformity. Soldiers would sell, or gamble with, excess clothing. Clothing was taken from the dead, sick, and discharged soldier and reissued. If anything was uniform about a Virginia soldier's clothing, especially early in the war, it might be a lack of uniformity.

As mentioned earlier, the documentation of the clothing worn by Virginia troops comes from three sources. One of these, deserter descriptions published in newspapers, usually lists the clothing of the deserter, his regiment, and often his company and, as the advertisement was the responsibility of the company captain, it included his captain's name. There are very few deserter advertisements. This gives, of course, a very small sample to illustrate the appearance of a particular regiment. The factors that led to diversity in uniforms, as stated above, suggest that deserter descriptions have limitations as resources and may or may not be accurate in describing the appearance of the soldier's comrades. State records provide a list of items issued but lack detailed descriptions. The numbers of breeches, shirts, and hats are given with occasional reference to type of material and/or color. These records include yardage of cloth issued to individual regiments and companies. This material was made into garments by soldiers with skill as tailors and by civilian contractors. Although this probably resulted in some uniformity, there would have been diversity due to the skill of the individual worker.

The third source of documentation is references gleaned from orders, letters, and journals. Often these include statements referring to the men being naked or ragtag. This may be misleading. A man in the eighteenth century without a coat was considered undressed. Also, exaggeration by an officer to insure supply was not unethical in the eighteenth-century military. These descriptions will be used with others to attempt to build a picture of the Virginia soldier.

In this section, each of the fifteen Virginia Line Regiments and the 1st and 2nd State Line Regiments will be examined. Also the Light Infantry Brigade of 1779 will be included, as Virginians were a substantial part of this special detachment. Since uniforms, at least early in the war, were unique to each regiment, the regiments must be looked at individually. The other equipment may be viewed as a whole. Also, as mentioned in the history, there was a renumbering of the Virginia Line in September 1779. The change in number is noted in the text. There was further consolidation the following year. From 1780 to the end of the war there is very little uniform or equipment documentation.

1ST VIRGINIA REGIMENT

The 1st Virginia Regiment was initially supplied by companies drawing equipment from the Williamsburg Public Store, October 1775-February 1776. Companies commanded by

John Green, William Davies, John Seayres, John Markham, Robert Ballard, John Fleming, William Campbell and George Gibson received supplies (Goodwin 1962:20-32, 44-45, 50, 52-61, 63, 65, 68). These nine companies would account for most, if not all, the personnel of the regiment.

The need for shoes was common with all companies except Gibson's. All companies, except Campbell's, received blue wool suitable for leggings. They received buttons which suggests they were making their own clothes and/or issued clothing came without buttons. Six of the eight companies received hats and material for hunting shirts. Five companies received shirts or the material to make shirts. Three companies received checked shirts. Three were issued stockings. It is possible that the cloth and buttons issued were delivered to a contractor for fabrication into uniforms, as was the case later in the war.

Markham's and Seayres' companies received green flannel. Markham got 87 yards and Seayres 86 3/4 yards. They also got 73 yards and 82 1/2 yards of oznaburg for breeches lining which suggests the end use for the green flannel (Goodwin 1962:30-31). Ballard's and Davies' companies received red duffle for "Capes and c.[such] for hunting shirts" (Goodwin 1962:32). There was some blue cloth and coating issued with no specifics as to end use.

The Williamsburg Public Store records show that the soldiers of the 1st Virginia appeared uniform in clothing as they marched north in 1776. The men wore hunting shirts probably of the same style and color, usually brown or some other dark color. They had blue wool leggings. Three companies, at least, had checked shirts. Their hats were probably the short brimmed round hat popular with light troops, although it is possible they wore a full military cocked hat. They wore the knee length breeches of the 18th century with coarse woolen stockings and the common shoe. Probably the men wore a wool or linen waistcoat.

The reference to "red duffle for capes and c." would suggest that the hunting shirt trim was of this material. Usually the collar and cuffs of a regimental coat contrasted with the body of the garment. A unique "facing" or "turned-up" color was a common method of individualizing a regiment's appearance. The term cape may mean a simple collar or a piece of material that spread over the shoulders as an added protection from the weather. This was a normal feature of some hunting shirts although it was usually made of linen. It would be unusual to use wool for a cape over linen but it would be very functional. The wool would provide warmth and better protection against rain than linen. The body of the hunting shirt, made of linen, would allow air circulation and the evaporation of perspiration.

This uniform did not compare with the standard European military fashion but it was an inexpensive and a very functional alternative. The upper body was protected by a heavy linen hunting shirt with, perhaps, an extra layer of material over the shoulders, a waistcoat underneath adding warmth. The hunting shirt or frock was an outer garment, usually made of stout material and extended to mid-thigh where it met the top of thick wool leggings. These protected the legs, breeches, and stockings from the damage caused by plants and grasses when off the road, and from undergrowth in the woods. The leggings also provided warmth and, by extending over the shoe tops, kept stones and such from getting into the shoes. The colors of these garments, blue, green and brown, provided a camouflage in the extensive forests of North America.

After the initial outfitting of the 1st Virginia—and this is the case with the regiments that follow—the Williamsburg Public Store records concerning individual regiments are of limited use. Only one entry for the regiment appears in 1777. Captain John Green received 16 hunting shirts and 73 pairs of leggings on April 12 (Goodwin 1962:120). The appearance of this regiment in later service with the Continental Army is found in deserter descriptions.

The *Virginia Gazette,* October 24, 1777, described a deserter from Lt. Francis Mennis' Company of the 1st Virginia as wearing a blue coat, white waistcoat and breeches, and white hat (Lefferts 1971:141). This is similar to an earlier advertisement in the *Gazette* on January 17, 1777, for a deserter

Joe Lee
96

FIGURE 1 - RIFLEMAN

from Captain Nelson's Company. This man had a blue regimental coat, faced red (collar, cuffs, lapels), white small clothes (waistcoat, breeches), and a white hat. This clothing shows a change from the frontier costume, described above, to that of a European soldier.

This uniform may not have been available to all, as suggested by the issue of hunting shirts and leggings to Capt. Green mentioned above. The *Virginia Gazette* ran an advertisement on May 23, 1777, for a deserter wearing a yellow hunting shirt. The color seems unusual in comparison to the dark colors usually chosen. This could be because of environmental effects on the garment dye. Another explanation might be that, with a year of field experience, this regiment chose a bright color feeling ready to meet the enemy in the open field. The concealment a dark color provided in the forest was no longer a concern.

In the autumn of 1778, recruits for the 1st Virginia were issued a suit of regimental clothes, a hat, two shirts, two pairs of stockings and two pairs of shoes (Goodwin 1962:146). This complied with a law for raising volunteers passed earlier that year. The suit of regimentals consisted of a coat, jacket, and breeches. The term jacket is not easily defined. This may be a waistcoat with sleeves, a garment used by British light troops and popular with both sides in the French and Indian War.

The troops already in the field were not neglected. The schooner, *May Flower,* was sent north at the end of October 1778, with a cargo containing 369 suits, 32 coats, seven jackets, and various pieces of cloth (Goodwin 1962:146-147). It is likely that this was not the only shipment, as it would have been insufficient for the entire Virginia Line.

These supplies may have gone directly to the army or may have been delivered to the Virginia Public Store in Philadelphia. In late 1778, and early 1779, the Public Store issued a tremendous amount of clothing and miscellaneous equipment to the individual regiments of the Virginia Line. In September 1778, the Line had been consolidated into 11 regiments and the 1st and 2nd Virginia State Line Regiments were sent to the Continental Army to partially make up for falling below the state's quota of fifteen regiments (Sellers 1978:49).

The records show the 1st Virginia received in September and October 1778, 456 pairs of shoes, 642 pairs of stockings, 238 soldier's shirts, 47 stocks, and 17 coats (PPS 1778-1779:9-11). The monthly strength report of this unit in October 1778, lists the regiment as having 279 officers and men on duty out of a total of 491 on the roster (Lesser 1976:88). The amount of equipment issued compared to the number of men on duty suggests that the men of this regiment were in need of supplies. Similar amounts of supplies issued to all the regiments at this time show the entire Virginia Line was probably "rag tag" in appearance in the summer of 1778, but became well uniformed by the spring of 1779.

The issue of specific items of clothing represents only part of the supplies received. The 1st Virginia also got scarlet, buff, and black cloth, thread, woolen caps, flannel waistcoats, cloth waistcoats, cloth breeches, stock buckles, coat buttons, vest buttons, and linen yard goods (PPS 1778-1779:9-11). Apparently the Army was producing its own clothing and receiving contracted uniforms.

It is also possible that the 1st Virginia and the other regiments that received equipment at this time were issued clothing produced in France. The French coat was blue or brown faced with red, waistcoats were red or blue, and breeches, red or green (Mollo 1975:193-194).

There is no specific documentation as to the 1st Virginia receiving clothing between the spring of 1779 and May 1780, when they surrendered with the garrison of Charleston, South Carolina. They left the main army with the other Virginia regiments in the autumn of 1779, and marched to Virginia where the Line was reorganized and the men were to receive supplies before marching for Charleston. The supply problems slowed the 1st Virginia's move south. They, and the 2nd Virginia, did not reach Charleston until April 1780 (Sellers 1978:62-63).

The 1st Regiment served as long as any Virginia military unit in the Revolution. There is no evidence to suggest that they were any better, or worse, supplied than any other unit.

Similarities in supply of other units with that of the 1st Virginia will allow reference to the description of this unit's clothing in type and source. This will avoid needless repetition.

2ND VIRGINIA REGIMENT

The records of the Williamsburg Public Store list equipment issued to the 2nd Virginia Regiment during the same period the 1st Virginia received supplies; late 1775 through early 1776. Six companies are mentioned in these lists, commanded by Captains George Johnson, Richard Parker, William Taliaferro, Richard Meade, Samuel Hawes, and William Fountain (Goodwin 1962:21, 27, 30, 32-34, 42-44, 46-50, 69, 75, 83). Since this unit received equipment from the same store and at the same time as the 1st Virginia, it is not surprising that the material is similar, as would be the appearance of the Regiment.

Five of the six companies received oznaburg for hunting shirts. The exception is William Fountain's Company which is noted as a rifle company (Goodwin 1962:47). The hunting shirt was a traditional item of clothing for the rifleman, therefore it is possible that Fountain's command came to Williamsburg with this garment. Also, two early deserter descriptions in the *Virginia Gazette* of September 6, 1776 and January 24, 1777, list brown hunting shirts (Lefferts 1971:141). This sample, although small, suggests a uniform color for this Regiment.

Five companies received stockings and three specifically blue hose. Four companies received shoes and four companies received hats. All the companies were issued blue material suitable for leggings. Hawes' Company got oznaburg for this purpose rather than wool (Goodwin 1962:75).

The style of these leggings is questionable. Two different styles were familiar to the Americans. During and after the French and Indian War period military fashion included a high legging, or full gaiter, made of heavy linen or wool, which extended from the shoe top to above the knee. This buttoned on the outside of the leg. A similar garment of leather or wool was worn by Native Americans that had sewn or laced seams rather than buttons. William Taliaferro's Company received horn buttons for leggings (Goodwin 1962:42). This suggests that the leggings were of the military variety.

Richard Meade's Company received 40 yards of oznaburg for breeches lining and 70 yards of flannel with no end use specified (Goodwin 1962:48). The flannel may have been for constructing breeches and the discrepancy between the yardage of flannel and oznaburg might be due to colonial garments not always being fully lined.

Documentation of the regiment's clothing between the initial Williamsburg issues and the 1778-1779 issues from the Philadelphia Store is, as with the 1st Virginia, limited to deserter descriptions. In January 1777, the *Virginia Gazette* ran advertisements for deserters from the 2nd Virginia. One man had a blue coat, the other a brown coat. One had brown linen trousers, the other buckskin. One had a flapped hat, the other a macaroni hat with a black band and silver buckle (Lefferts 1971:141-142). This is a small sample but it suggests a lack of uniformity in contrast to the troops that marched North.

The *Pennsylvania Packet* on March 11, 1778, gives a deserter description. The man has a blue coat with blue velvet collar, green waistcoat, buckskin breeches, and a round hat. The velvet collar is out of the ordinary, however, the blue coat does match the coats of three deserters mentioned in a deserter description on September 5, 1777. These coats had white binding (Lefferts 1971:141).

The 2nd Virginia, like the 1st, benefited from the material shipped from Williamsburg in the autumn of 1778. They received a substantial amount of equipment from the Philadelphia Store (PPS 1778-1779:11-12). Like the other units it probably was the last major supply received before the surrender at Charleston (Sellers 1978:62).

The material issued from the store at Philadelphia included numerous shoes, stockings, shirts, hats, and caps. Linen, other cloth, buttons and thread were issued (PPS 1778-1779:11-12). The new clothing would help make the winter more comfortable, however, the issue of neck stocks shows a soldierly appearance would be required.

The 2nd Virginia's appearance did not greatly differ from the other regiments of the Virginia Line. The white binding on the coats, mentioned above, instead of coats "turned up" with a contrasting color was unique. Yet, during most of the war the 2nd Virginia probably suffered shortages and benefited when supplies were adequate with their fellow Virginians.

3RD VIRGINIA REGIMENT

Documentary evidence concerning the 3rd Virginia is limited. The Williamsburg records refer to only one company of this regiment, commanded by John Chilton. Chilton received oznaburg for hunting shirts and blue half-thick, a wool material suitable for leggings (Goodwin 1962:41). This issue was during the same period the 1st and 2nd Regiments received supplies and suggests the 3rd Virginia's appearance might be the same as these other units.

The *Pennsylvania Packet* of September 5, 1778, provides the only deserter description for this regiment. Two men left wearing light blue drab coats with pale blue facings, green vests, and linen overalls (Lefferts 1971:142). The green vests, which also appear in the 2nd regiment, suggest uniformity. The overalls, like the hunting shirt, are a very functional piece of clothing combining breeches and leggings into one garment.

The 3rd Virginia received a large quantity of supplies from the Philadelphia Store in 1778-1779. They were issued shoes and shoe buckles, stockings, shirts, coats, wool and linen vests, wool caps, and stocks and buckles. They got linen and wool cloth, thread and buttons (PPS n.d.: 13-14). The need to manufacture their own clothes, as others were doing, suggests the needs of this regiment were those faced by the other units of the Virginia Line.

4TH VIRGINIA REGIMENT

The 4th Virginia is represented in the Williamsburg Store record by a single company commanded by John Brent. They received oznaburg for hunting shirts and blue coating that may have been for leggings (Goodwin 1962:71). This documentation is augmented by an early deserter description in the *Virginia Gazette* on September 27, 1776. This man is described as having a hunting shirt faced with red, checked shirt, and trousers (Lefferts 1971:142). The red facing refers to collar and cuffs and corresponds to the evidence cited in the discussion of the 1st Virginia.

The Philadelphia Store records lists the 4th Virginia as receiving the same type of supplies as the other units, stockings, shoes, stocks, shirts, coats, wool caps, shoe buckles, flannel waistcoats, cloth breeches, and hats. The 4th also received cloth, linen, thread, and coat and vest buttons (PPS 1778-1779:14-15).

5TH VIRGINIA REGIMENT

The 5th Virginia Regiment appears in the Williamsburg Store record as of March 4, 1776 when Captain George Stubblefield received oznaburg for hunting shirts and leggings (Goodwin 1962:70). Two other companies are recorded. John Pleasant received coating and frieze for leggings and Ralph Faulkner was issued blue hose (Goodwin 1962:76,77). The 5th became part of the 3rd Virginia during the September 1778 reorganization of the Virginia Line.

6TH VIRGINIA REGIMENT

The 6th Virginia Regiment is better documented than other regiments. An orderly book contains the following regimental order dated April 3, 1776.

The Captains of the 6th Battalion, together with the other Officers, are immediately to provide themselves with Hunting Shirts, short and fringed; the men's shirts are to be short and plain, the Sergeants' shirts to have small white cuffs and plain; The Drummers shirts to be with dark cuffs. Both Officers and Soldiers to have Hats cut round and bound with black; The Brims of their Hat's to be two inches deep and cocked on one, with a button and loop and cockades, which is to be worn on the left. Neither men nor Officers to do duty in any other Uniform. The Officers and soldiers are to wear their hair short and as near a like as possible (Goodwin 1962:11).

The Williamsburg Public Store supplied five companies of the 6th Virginia from March 4, 1776, through September 14, 1776. The companies were commanded by William Gregory, James Johnson, Thomas Massie, Samuel Cabell, and Oliver Towles (Goodwin 1962:70, 74-75, 77, 81-82, 89, 93-96). A deserter description in the *Virginia Gazette*, May 10, 1776, refers to a company commanded by Thomas Hutchings (Lefferts 1971:142). Hutching's company is not mentioned in the Williamsburg Public Store record.

The Williamsburg record and deserter descriptions do not completely support the uniformity called for in the regimental order quoted above. Gregory's and Johnson's companies received oznaburg for hunting shirts, however, Towles' received close-bodied coats and jackets (Goodwin 1962:74, 89, 96).

Deserter descriptions from the same period suggest a variety of clothing. The deserters from Hutching's company had the following clothing:

hunting shirt dyed black
blue duffle coat
blue leggings
black and white mixed Virginia cloth coat and waistcoat
copperas striped coat and waistcoat of Virginia cloth
light colored kersey coat
leather breeches (Lefferts 1971:142-143).

Deserters from Samuel Cabell's Company were described in the *Virginia Gazette*, July 5, 1776, as having,

new suit of gray broadcloth
hunting shirts trimmed in red [two examples]
leather breeches
breeches of light colored sagathy (Lefferts 1971:142)

Later in the year, October 18, 1776, the *Virginia Gazette* described two deserters from the 6th Virginia:

snuff colored coat and waistcoat
silver button and loop to his hat
dark colored hunting shirt
striped Virginia cloth coat and waistcoat
russia drab breeches

The variety of clothing in these descriptions and that supplied from the Williamsburg Public Store does not support compliance with the order of April 3, 1776. The Public Store did issue shoes to four of the five companies and four of the five received leather breeches.

The leather breeches appear again in a deserter description in the *Virginia Gazette*, November 8, 1776. Two of the three men mentioned had leather breeches, all have hunting shirts trimmed red and one has a gray broadcloth waistcoat (Lefferts 1971:143). The waistcoat description is the same as the deserter from Cabell's Company mentioned above. The gray colored material appears again in a deserter description in the *Pennsylvania Packet*, May 13, 1778. This man had a light gray coat with green facings, a gray waistcoat, oznaburg overalls, and a small round hat with a piece of bear fur on it (Mollo 1975:176). The 6th Virginia was incorporated into the 2nd Virginia during the 1778 reorganization of the Virginia Line.

7TH VIRGINIA REGIMENT

The Williamsburg Public Store record provides much information concerning the clothing of the 7th Virginia. Four companies were recorded as receiving supplies. These companies were commanded by Gregory Smith, Holt Richardson, Charles Tomkies, and Joseph Crockett (Goodwin 1962:73, 75-76, 80, 86, 89, 103). Another company, commanded by Nathanial Cocke, is mentioned in a deserter description in the May 10, 1776, Supplement to the *Virginia Gazette*.

Two of the four companies received oznaburg for hunting shirts. The deserter description mentions two men with dark colored hunting shirts and a third with a hunting shirt of Virginia striped cloth dyed almost black. This dark color appears in a later deserter description in the *Virginia Gazette*, April 4, 1776 (Lefferts 1971:143).

Other clothing items issued to the 7th Virginia in Williamsburg include hats, cloth for breeches, buttons, shoes, and coating for leggings. Tomkie's Company received twenty coats (Goodwin 1962:96). It is unclear if this meant a uniform coat. The deserter description of May 10 mentions a snuff colored coat (Lefferts 1971:143). This may be a similar garment.

The regiment's commander, Colonel William Dangerfield, received a large amount of supplies from the Williamsburg store on May 13, 1776. It would not be unusual in eighteenth-century military operations for a regimental commander to be charged with equipment issued to his men. This is, however, unique to the Williamsburg record due to the large amount of supplies. Dangerfield received,

425 yards drilling
504 yards check
252 yards white linen
159 1/2 yards stripes
159 1/2 yards stripes
174 yards white sheeting
96 3/4 yards douls
836 1/4 yards oznaburg
80 felt hats
248 pair shoes
4 pieces cotton 82 yards
24 dutch blankets best kind
4 lb. brown thread

3 lb. brown thread
2 lb. ditto
1 1/2 lb. nuns thread
8 yards duck (Goodwin 1962:86).

The 836 1/4 yards of oznaburg would produce 152 hunting shirts at 5 1/2 yards per shirt. This would be a sufficient supply for three companies, using the desired number of 50 men per company. If the material issued to the companies mentioned earlier is included, this would have been sufficient to provide hunting shirts to the entire regiment.

A question is raised, however, due to the two issues of Virginia striped cloth to Dangerfield. The deserter description, mentioned earlier, describes a hunting shirt of Virginia striped cloth dyed almost black. If Virginia cloth was used for hunting shirts the oznaburg may have been used for leggings. This was not uncommon. Since Dangerfield was not issued any heavy wool cloth, the heavier linen, oznaburg, may have become leggings. The fact that two companies of the 7th received coating for leggings in an earlier issue would support the belief that heavy wool was not available.

The goods issued to the 7th Virginia suggest they could leave Williamsburg with a uniform appearance. Yet, by the spring of 1777, this uniformity was probably gone. The *Virginia Gazette* printed two deserter descriptions on April 4 that suggests a much different appearance for the regiment. One describes a man wearing a uniform coat of pale blue turned up with red calmanico. The other, which covers four deserters, lists dark colored hunting shirts, red waistcoat, light colored coarse cloth coat, and brown frieze leggings. This description specifies that one man's hunting shirt is fringed around the capes, ruffles, tail, and down the breast (Lefferts 1971:143). This is much more elaborate than the plain garment called for in the Regimental Order of the 6th Virginia. This also strongly suggests, due to the fringe running down the breast, that this hunting shirt (or frock) was of the variety that was open in the front rather than a pullover shirt.

In the Philadelphia issue of 1778-1779, the 7th, now renumbered the 5th Virginia, like its fellow units, received shirts, wool caps, cloth breeches, red waistcoats, waistcoats [no color specified], breeches, flannel waistcoats, stockings, stocks and buckles, hats, and shoe buckles. This is the only regiment that did not receive shoes. They also received linen, cloth, thread, and buttons (PPS 1778-1779:15-16).

8TH VIRGINIA REGIMENT

General Charles Lee stated on August 2, 1776, that the 8th Virginia was the best armed, clothed, and equipped for immediate service (Sanchez-Saavedra 1978:56). A deserter description of this period describes the man as wearing a hunting shirt, breeches, and flapped hat (Lefferts 1971:143). Lee was a former British army officer. He was familiar with the standard appearance of a European army. Lee's statement, with the deserter description specifying the "regular" American uniform, indicates that the equipment was the best that could be provided by the authorities in Virginia.

Only one issue to the 8th Virginia appears in the Williamsburg Public Store record. The regiment's commander, John Peter Gabriel Muhlenberg, received the following supplies on May 11, 1776:

432 yards drilling
79 yards Ravs. duck
504 yards check
240 yards white linen
316 yards blue stripe
174 yards white sheeting
36 yards brown sheeting
80 yards douls
872 1/2 yards oznaburg
19 small blankets (Goodwin 1962:85)

The oznaburg probably was intended for hunting shirts. The check was for shirts. The other material it can be assumed was made up into breeches, waistcoats, and perhaps leggings.

Any uniformity suggested by the Williamsburg issues or Lee's statement seems to have been gone by 1777. Separate deserter advertisements appeared in the *Pennsylvania Packet* for men from the same company. One advertisement, May 6, 1777, described the man as having a hunting shirt, blue waistcoat, blue germantown milled stockings, and a macaroni beaver hat. The other advertisement, August 19, 1777, lists the clothing as a short blue coat, linen jacket, breeches, and thread stockings (Lefferts 1971:143). The 8th Virginia was incorporated into the 4th Virginia in the 1778 reorganization of the Virginia Line.

9TH VIRGINIA REGIMENT

The 9th Virginia Regiment is represented in the Williamsburg Public Store record by two companies commanded by James Innis and Samuel Woodson (Goodwin 1962:71-72, 79-80). On March 29, 1776, Woodson was issued 370 yards of oznaburg for hunting and body shirts. The use of the heavy oznaburg for body shirts suggests that lighter weight linen was unavailable. Shortages might also be shown by Woodson receiving frieze and coating for leggings. The coarse frieze was a usual legging material but the coating was of lighter weight and greater cost and would not normally be used for this purpose. Woodson also received hats, shoes, and socks. Innis was issued a variety of material including broad cloth, frieze, douls and coating. He also got shoes and hose.

The only deserter description appeared in the *Pennsylvania Packet*, April 15, 1777. The deserter, from Captain Levin Joynes' Company, was wearing a light brown coat with red facings (Lefferts 1971:144). The 9th Virginia became part of the 1st Virginia in the reorganization of the Virginia Line in September 1778.

10TH VIRGINIA REGIMENT

The 10th Virginia Regiment does not appear in the Williamsburg Public Store records. There is only one deserter description. This description from 1777, lists the man, from Captain Thomas West's Company, as wearing a hunting shirt, drawers, and leggings (Lefferts 1971:144).

The 10th Virginia, renumbered the 6th Virginia, was in as much need as the other regiments in the autumn of 1778. Between September 25 and February 2, the 6th received shirts, stockings, shoes, woolen caps, soldiers hats, stocks and stock buckles. They also received linen, wool cloth, thread, and buttons (PPS 1778-1779:16-17).

11TH VIRGINIA REGIMENT

The commander of the 11th Virginia Regiment was Daniel Morgan. Morgan was best known for his association with the use of riflemen throughout the war. It has been assumed that Morgan's regiment contained many riflemen probably wearing the traditional dress of riflemen including the hunting shirt (Higginbotham 1961:56-57). A deserter description for the 11th does little to confirm or refute this assumption. Two men left James Calderwood's Company wearing long, light colored coats and jackets (Lefferts 1971:144). These may be hunting shirts as these garments have been illustrated as knee length.

The Philadelphia Public Store records show that the 11th Virginia, now renumbered as the 7th Virginia, did not receive supplies until January 7, 1779, which is later than other regiments of the Virginia Line. The supplies the regiment received do not suggest that they were any less in need. They were issued brown linen, cloth, thread, and buttons. In clothing they received red cloth waistcoats, cloth breeches, woolen caps, stocks and buckles, shoes, and shirts (PPS 1778-1779:18).

The issues to this regiment were recorded in January and February 1779, and are of lesser quantities than other units.

This is probably due to the regiment mustering less than 60 officers and men fit for duty during those months, as most of the regiment was on furlough (Lesser 1976:100, 104).

12TH VIRGINIA REGIMENT

The 12th Virginia is not mentioned in the Williamsburg records. Documentation of this regiment's uniform before the issue in Philadelphia comes from deserter descriptions. Captain William Vause lost five men. The descriptions in the *Pennsylvania Packet*, August 13 and 19, 1777, lists three of the men wearing hunting shirts and leather breeches. One man wore a hunting shirt and trousers or overalls, and the last man, hunting shirt, trousers and a small round hat. The *Pennsylvania Packet* of August 19 also lists a deserter from Michael Bowyer's Company wearing a coarse linen frock and overalls (Lefferts 1971:144). This coarse linen frock may be a hunting shirt, the difference due to terminology used by the company commander or an army clerk.

The 12th Virginia, renumbered the 8th Virginia in the reorganization of September 1778, received a large amount of equipment from the Philadelphia Public Store in late 1778-early 1779. They were issued flannel and cloth waistcoats, cloth breeches, shoes, stockings, shirts, woolen caps, coats, stocks, and hats. Like the other regiments, the 8th received wool and linen material, thread, and buttons (PPS 1778-1779:19-20).

13TH VIRGINIA REGIMENT

The 13th Virginia does not appear in the Williamsburg Public Store record. Deserter descriptions do, however, provide a small sample that suggests uniformity in this unit. The companies of James Neal and Davis Steele placed advertisements in the *Pennsylvania Packet* on April 22, 1777, and July 15, 1777, and in the *Pennsylvania Evening Post* on August 16, 1777. Each description includes a blue regimental coat cuffed or faced with yellow (Lefferts 1971:144). The reason one description specifies cuff color and another facing may be due to the individual who wrote the advertisement or perhaps slight variation in uniform coats.

The entire 13th Virginia was sent to garrison Fort Pitt in May 1778, however, part of the regiment was there as early as April 1777. (Lesser 1971:70. Kellogg 1916:411). The regiment was redesignated the 9th Virginia in the reorganization of September 1778. The 9th Virginia is not listed in the Philadelphia Store record, undoubtedly because of its frontier location. Apparently, they could have used the supplies.

(Col. Daniel Brodhead to Gen. George Washington:)

There is a prodigious deficiency of Clothing & Money in this Department [Western Department], some Cloth has indeed been purchased in the State of Virginia, but the means of making it up are not provided; Shoes and Linnen cannot be had at any rate unless they are sent up by the Clothier Genl. (and I am wearied with making fruitless applications to him and the Board of War, although) the troops are full of Vermin (Kellogg 1916:271).

14TH VIRGINIA REGIMENT

The only record of the 14th Virginia directly receiving supplies from Williamsburg is 300 pair of hose on April 9, 1777 (Goodwin 1962:119). A deserter description in the *Virginia Gazette*, July 4, 1777, suggests that the need was greater than stockings. Nathan Reid's Company lost two men, one wearing a striped cotton fly coat and waistcoat, linen drawers, and leggings. The other man had a white hunting shirt, leather leggings and moccasins (Lefferts 1971:144).

The 14th Virginia, renumbered the 10th Virginia in the reorganization of September 1778, received considerable supplies from the Philadelphia Public Store between September 1778 and February 1779. They were issued shoes, stockings, shirts, woolen caps, breeches, waistcoats, hats, stocks, and stock buckles. They also received cloth, linen, thread, and buttons (PPS 1778-1779:20-21).

15TH VIRGINIA REGIMENT

The 15th Virginia regiment appears in the Williamsburg store record with an issue to one soldier on November 24, 1778. He received a regimental suit, 10 1/2 yards of check, two pairs of hose, two pairs of shoes, and a hat (Goodwin 1962:150). The yardage of check would be sufficient for two shirts. This issue was made just when this regiment was receiving supplies in Philadelphia. It is likely that the men with the Army received similar supplies.

In 1778, the Philadelphia Store issued to the 15th Virginia, now the 11th Virginia, the same equipment issued to the other units. They received cloth breeches, flannel and cloth waistcoats, stockings, woolen caps, stocks and buckles, shirts, and hats. Like the other units, they received cloth, linen thread, and buttons (PPS 1778-1779:22).

1ST VIRGINIA STATE LINE REGIMENT

The 1st Virginia State Line Regiment appears in the Williamsburg Public Store record beginning March 15, 1777. Five companies and the regiment, through the commander, received hose, shoes, checked shirts, and hats. Besides this clothing, they got oznaburg, sheeting, shalloon (a light wool used for coat lining), thread, and buttons (Goodwin 1962:112, 115, 118-121, 123-124, 129, 155-156).

Deserter descriptions from this period do not suggest that the Williamsburg Store material produced a uniform appearance. An advertisement in the *Virginia Gazette*, May 2, 1777, lists a striped Virginia cloth coat and breeches. On June 6, 1777, the *Gazette* advertised for a man wearing a short striped

FIGURE 2 - REGULAR

jacket. The *Gazette* of June 27, 1777, lists a light colored coat and breeches (Lefferts 1971:145).

The 1st State Line Regiment was serving with the Continental Army during the autumn 1778 and the winter/spring 1779. Therefore, they received the issue of equipment from the Philadelphia Store. Not unlike the Virginia Continental Line regiments they received stockings, shoes, shirts, coats, stocks and buckles, woolen caps, hats, waistcoats, and breeches. They also received cloth, linen thread, and buttons (PPS 1778-1779:23-24).

It is important to note that this regiment received much the same equipment as the other units, as a deserter description in the spring provides an excellent view of the uniform that may have been a result of the supplies issued from Philadelphia. The deserter wore a blue coat turned up red, red waistcoat, and breeches. This is the uniform specified in regulations. It can be assumed with some confidence that this was the appearance of the entire Virginia Line in the Spring of 1779.

2ND VIRGINIA STATE LINE REGIMENT

The 2nd Virginia State Line Regiment received their first issue from the Williamsburg Store in March 1777 (Goodwin 1962:115). Three companies received shoes and a variety of cloth and linen. Benjamin Spiller's Company received cloth specifically for coats and jackets and red cloth for facings (Goodwin 1962:136). Robert Lovell's Company was issued blue frieze for coats and large plain buttons (Goodwin 1962:141). It seems obvious the regiment was manufacturing, or having manufactured, blue coats faced red, the desired uniform for the Virginia soldier.

This model uniform is supported by a deserter description that appeared in the *Virginia Gazette*, September 5, 1777. The soldier, from John Dudley's Company, lists a blue coat turned up red (Lefferts 1971:145). This advertisement, only four months after the issue from the Williamsburg Stores, suggests this soldier is probably wearing the coat he received in Williamsburg.

The 2nd Virginia State Line Regiment received a substantial quantity of equipment from the Philadelphia Store in 1778-1779. They were issued shoes, stockings, shirts, neck stocks and buckles, waistcoats, hats, woolen caps, breeches, and coats. They received cloth, linen, thread, and buttons (PPS 1778-1779:24-25). Their need was equal with the other units. This shows that the Williamsburg issued supplies could not withstand a full year of wear and tear. The winter of 1777-1778 was spent at Valley Forge and many accounts of the soldiers' appearance during that winter suggests that the equipment, new in the spring, was now no better than rags in the winter. This provides a hint as to the longevity of uniform clothing of the Virginia soldier.

THE CORPS OF LIGHT INFANTRY, 1779

Virginia Line regiments supplied a large portion of the Light Infantry Brigade during the 1779 campaign and documentation of this service is important to the discussion of the uniforms of the Virginia soldier. In the Continental Army each regiment was to designate one company as its light company. It was composed of the best soldiers: elite troops. During the campaign season the light infantry companies of the line regiments were combined into a special corps.

The Light Infantry would be recognized on the field by modifications to the regular uniform. The coat may have been shorter than the regulation coat and the cocked hat of the regular would be replaced by a leather cap decorated with a horsehair plume or other device. American equipment shortages prevented major uniform changes. However, it seems the commander, Anthony Wayne, attempted to make the appearance of the Corps unique and this caused problems for the Virginians.

The Virginians had received caps as members of the Light Corps but they fell short of regulations. The orderly book of the 1st Regiment of the Corps states on October 22, 1779,

FIGURE 3 - LIGHT INFANTRYMAN

General Wayne has observed with great concern that the Virginians are the only troops in the Light Infantry that has not procured hair for their caps (Gamble 1892:250).

The concern for a properly decorated cap seems a small problem, as the 1st Regiment's orderly book states on September 30, 1779, that barefoot men are to be returned to the Army (Gamble 1892:256). This suggests that the shoes issued in quantity to the Virginians in early 1779 did not hold up for a campaign season.

The documentation shows that the Virginia Regiments that served with the Continental Army received equal treatment from the state regarding clothing supplies. It also seems that the state attempted to provide the regulation uniform and, if that were not possible, tried to see the men had something in terms of clothing.

Where there are differences in uniforms between regiments the variety can be attributed to the location of the unit when supplies were available. Yet, even within a unit there was variation. A regiment viewed at two hundred yards might seem uniform, at ten yards it would be apparent that no two men were alike. Differences in uniform color, cut, fabric, quality of construction, and personal modification was probably the norm.

If the documentation would allow, each company should be studied. Individual companies might be assigned to duty away from their regiments. This may have allowed them to get clothing that the rest of the regiment would not receive. Also, the detached company could possibly miss receiving an issue made available to their regiment during their absence. This detached service may have caused more, or perhaps less, wear on the clothes than that experienced by the remainder of the unit.

Soldiers individually bought, sold, traded, and gambled for extra clothing. An issue of a new garment might require the soldier to produce a worn item to prove need. A competent "scrounger" might be well dressed and the individual next to him in the ranks might be in rags.

The appearance of the Virginia soldier in the Revolution changed over time. To understand how he was clothed several variables must be specified such as what period of the war and which regiment. The state of Virginia made every effort to equip her soldiers. There were times that clothing was adequate in quantity, and times of hardship. This hardship may be magnified through twentieth-century eyes.

EXAMPLES OF CLOTHING

HUNTING SHIRTS (FIGURE 1)

Hunting shirt is the term used in most of the documentation to describe a simple outer garment for the upper part of the body. The term rifle shirt, rifle frock, or hunting frock may appear in primary or secondary sources to describe an identical garment. The hunting shirt was subject to modification using a combination of three major characteristics: length, fringe, and front opening, as opposed to a pullover shirt. Despite the design the function remained the same.

Virginia, at the beginning of the Revolution, was unable to provide the soldiers with the standard military coat and the hunting shirt was substituted (Goodwin 1962:viii-ix). It was retained after regimental coats were supplied and probably worn when the soldier was off duty or engaged in fatigue duty such as building fortifications. It was simple to construct, comfortable, and if dyed a dark color, it would provide the soldier with camouflage in the woods. The hunting shirt was recognized as the common dress of riflemen and this had an additional benefit. Washington urged its adoption because of its practicality and economy, and because "it is a dress which is justly supposed to carry no small terror to the enemy, who think every such person a complete marksman" (Huddleston 1978:16).

The hunting shirt can be documented as being used by twelve of the fifteen Virginia Line Regiments. It can be assumed that the remaining three had the garment. The 11th Virginia, not mentioned in the documentation as having hunting shirts, was commanded by Daniel Morgan. Morgan was best known for commanding special rifle detachments, and it seems likely that at least some men of his regiment would have been riflemen and/or dressed like riflemen. The other regiments who are not mentioned as receiving hunting shirts are the 13th and 15th Virginia. These regiments were raised during the same period as the 12th and 14th regiments who were issued this garment or the linen material for its construction (Lefferts 1971:144). It seems likely that the 13th and 15th Regiments received a similar issue.

Although it is clear that hunting shirts were used by soldiers of the Virginia Line, details concerning the style are vague, limited, usually, to color. Yellow appeared on a member of the 1st Virginia, brown on a soldier of the 2nd, black in the 6th, almost black in the 7th, and white in the 14th (VG, May 23, 1777; Lefferts 1971:141-144).

In at least some instances, material of contrasting colors was used on the collars/capes and cuffs to provide a specific identity to individual regiments. Red wool was issued to the 1st Virginia for this purpose (Goodwin 1962:32). The hunting shirts of the 6th Regiment were to have white cuffs for sergeants and dark cuffs for drummers (Goodwin 1962:11).

The length and decoration, like the color, varied from unit to unit. The 6th Virginia was to have a short, plain shirt (Goodwin 1962:711). The 7th Virginia had at least one member with a fringed shirt (Lefferts 1971:143). The apparent variety in this garment prohibits a single model for illustration.

To describe this garment it will be divided into two types, hunting shirt and hunting frock. The hunting shirt is a garment opened only a short distance in the front at the collar and is put on over the head. The hunting, or rifle, frock is open in front for its full length and is put on like a jacket.

The first variable characteristic is length. The frock may have been short, extending only to the hips, or may have terminated below the knees. The shirt, not open in front, would probably have been mid-thigh length at the extreme. If it were any longer, it would have constricted movement.

The second variable is the use of capes and fringe. These elements could have been used on either type, depending on regulations, availability of material, and personal preference. Although there is a decorative aspect to capes and fringe, they also served a functional purpose. The capes gave extra protection to the shoulders and the fringe helped "channel" the water from the garment, acting like a wick.

Also of interest is that the garment is from a civilian rather than a military tradition. This is revealed in the narrative of a Massachusetts militiaman, Simeon Alexander, in his pension application. He comments on Daniel Morgan's riflemen. His reference to Morgan's command should not be understood to be the 11th Virginia. Morgan, at this time, was leading a company of riflemen whom he had recruited and marched north to join the army besieging the British in Boston.

The uniform of Morgan's regiment was a short frock made of pepper-and-salt colored cotton cloth like a common frock worn by our country people, except that it was short and open before, to be tied with strings, pantaloons of the same fabric and color, and some kind of cap, but I do not now remember as to its form (Dann 1980:106).

It is doubtful that the material was cotton. Oznaburg, a coarse linen material, is regularly mentioned as the material of choice for hunting shirts or frocks. The reference to the garment being short should not suggest that this was usual. Four illustrations of the period showing soldiers in frocks depict one as waist length, two mid-thigh, and one below the knee (Huddleston 1978:62-64, 66).

Perhaps the only surviving example of a Revolutionary War rifle frock is at the Washington Headquarters Museum, Newburgh, New York. It is illustrated in the *Sketchbook '76*; and its construction, and, the speculation of the author concerning other hunting shirts, is described as follows.

The body was made of one piece of fine linen, folded at the shoulder with an opening cut for the neck and front-gussets were set in the neck opening and the opening was then gathered to fit the collar-the cape was then stitched on where the collar joins the body-buttons were cloth covered wood, or of bone or pewter. Fringe was made by cutting strips of linen, then by pulling out the threads on both edges, and folding the strip down the center-fringe was added or omitted to suit the wearer or any regulations in force. The pleated or plain sleeve was made with a gusset set in the underside where it joins the body. The cuff is sewn inside the sleeve and has a button and loop-descriptions seem to indicate the shirts were made in many colors-white, black, blue, brown, grey, ash, and shades of green (Klinger 1967:17).

The pleated sleeves may be an exception rather than a rule. It is doubtful if the Virginians regularly used such an elaborate version of this garment. This example does, however, present all the components of a frock.

WAISTCOAT (Figure 2)

The waistcoat worn by the Virginia soldier, like the other items of clothing, probably did not differ substantially from the civilian garment. Although waistcoats were also made of linen, the records indicate that the waistcoats most often issued to the Virginia troops were made of wool, either broadcloth or flannel. The use of wool would provide warmth if wool coats were not available and the men used hunting shirts as an outer garment.

Deserter descriptions include waistcoats of a variety of colors. The Philadelphia Store Records, however, and descriptions of deserters from units that would have been supplied from military stores in Virginia, show that red was the standard color of issue. The Philadelphia records also list vest buttons as issued. This could mean the waistcoats were issued without buttons or that the linen and wool material issued was being made up into waistcoats.

An illustration of a waistcoat based upon surviving specimens of garments worn by Generals Washington and Gansevoort appears in *Sketchbook '76*. It is close-fitting to the body. It is constructed of four main pieces; two make up the back, and two the front. There are pocket flaps on each side that may or may not have been functional (Klinger 1967:7-8). A regular soldier's waistcoat was not constructed of as fine a material as that of an officer. The waistcoat closed with approximately a dozen buttons.

BREECHES, OVERALLS, TROUSERS (Figures 2 & 3)

The Virginia soldier undoubtedly had access to, and used, trousers and overalls during the Revolution, but the documentation would suggest that breeches were, by far, the most common. They were manufactured from linen, buckskin, and wool (both broadcloth and flannel). The colors included red, brown, buff, green, and blue.

The style of the breeches was that of civilian garments. Trousers and overalls were similar in construction except they terminated at the ankle rather than the knee. Each of these garments had a wide waistband that buttoned in front and was adjusted to fit using laces in the rear that were tied. There was a wide flap, or fall, in the front that buttoned at the waistband. The seat was full; the extra material allowed the wearer to sit as these garments were fitted close to the leg and buckled tight at the knee to hold the stockings. A leg garter consisting of a narrow leather band, buckled over the material, served the same purpose with trousers and overalls.

Trousers and overalls differed at the ankle. The trousers ended at this point with a simple hem. The overalls reached below the opening of the shoe and a tongue or flap was added to the front to cover the shoe. A strap ran under the arch of the shoe to hold the leg of the overalls down and they were fastened tight at the ankle with buttons along the outside seam. This, in effect, replaced the full or half gaiters, protecting the leg and preventing stones and other matter from getting into the shoe.

SHIRT

The shirt was not unlike the basic hunting shirt discussed elsewhere, the major difference was the weight of the fabric.

White or natural color linen, plain or checked, was cut into rectangular pieces consisting of the body, sleeves, collar, cuffs, and gussets. Intended to be loose fitting, except at the collar and cuffs, the construction was simple.

> The main body of the early shirt is made from one length of fabric. Sometimes the warp direction of this piece runs vertically up the front, over the shoulders, and down the back; there is no shoulder seam-only a fold-and the lower edge of the shirt must be hemmed. There are two side seams where the fabric is joined from the underarm region to the hem. Not infrequently both edges of the fabric are selvage, indicating that the material was utilized at full loom width. In many shirts a single piece of material was wrapped horizontally around the body. With this arrangement there is generally but one seam, the lower edge often is a selvage, and a shoulder seam is necessary. With either method of construction, a reinforcement of extra fabric from the sleeve top to collar was sometime used.
>
> To this basic length of fabric forming the shirt body were attached two additional rectangles for the sleeves, smaller rectangles for the collar and cuffs and a full complement of gussets which, with strategically placed gathers, provided ease and fit. This basic format readily lent itself to variations in size, length, fullness, fabric type and width, and embellishment as dictated by the size and personal preference of the wearer, its intended use for work or dress, slight local variations, and availability of fabric. Not all the characteristics found in the Pennsylvania shirts described are by any means exclusive to this state or even to America (Gehret 1976:99).

Although the description above is of shirts found in Pennsylvania, it would probably be applicable to most eighteenth-century shirts. Nor is there any evidence that the shirts used by Virginia soldiers would have been other than this type, the material and design of which was taken from the civilian traditions. The term "soldier shirt" or "officer shirt" found in the Philadelphia Store Record probably suggests the quality of the fabric and the use of embellishments rather than a different style.

HEADGEAR (Figures 1, 2, & 3)

The headgear worn by the Virginia soldier can be divided into three types: hats, caps, and woolen knitted caps. The hat is constructed from felt and has a brim of varying width that extends the entire circumference of the crown. The general shape of the cap resembles a modern baseball cap. It is of leather with a brim over the eyes. Also, these may have been made from a felt hat with brim removed except in the front. The woolen knitted cap is similar to the modern winter stocking cap and descends from a very old folk tradition.

The infantry soldier's hat of the eighteenth century was fashioned from felt with a low, rounded crown. The brim was cut to a specific width and turned up, or cocked, according to regulation or personal preference. The style most frequently found in the military of the period was a hat turned up on three sides (Figure 4a), not unlike the tricorn, or three-cornered hat, common to the civilian population. The major difference is that the military cocked hat was turned up slightly off center in the front that brought the front point of the hat over the left eye rather than the nose of the wearer, which was the case with its civilian counterpart. This allows a flat side of the hat to align perpendicular to the soldier's left shoulder. The military drill of the period called for the musket to be carried on the left shoulder, which would have caused the civilian tricorn hat to interfere with the movement of the musket. The military cocked hat was decorated with a button and loop on the left side, a cord that ran around the base of the brim, and a cockade. The edges of the brim were covered, or bound, with a narrow piece of cloth.

There were other treatments of the soldier's hat. One style, apparently popular with Virginians early in the war, was the round hat (Figure 1). This variety is illustrated by an order to the 6th Virginia Regiment:

> Both officers and soldiers to have hats cut round and bound in black; the brims of their hats to be 2 inches deep and cocked on one side, with a button and loop and cockades, which is to be worn on the left (Goodwin 1962:11).

Another treatment that appears in at least one deserter description is the flopped or flapped hat, which is simply a hat with the brim left wide and unturned.

The basic hat may have had the brim cut off at the bottom edge of the crown except a few inches in front. The remaining brim, of what was then a cap, might now be turned up and hooked to the crown. Common terms for this cap were jockey or light infantryman's cap. This variety of cap was also manufactured from leather with a brim perpendicular to the crown (Figure 3). Another piece of leather, called a shield, mounted vertically in front of the crown, was fixed to the cap at the junction of the crown and brim. The shield may have been painted along the edge with the regimental number in Roman numerals. Some varieties have decorative metal chains, horsehair plumes, and/or a cloth band, or turban, tied around the crown (Neumann and Kravic 1975:137).

This hat was usually reserved for elite troops such as light infantry. It was worn by the Virginians attached to the light infantry corps of the Continental Army during the campaign of 1779. The Virginian's cap did not have a hair plume (Gamble 1892:250). Any other decoration would be speculation.

The Philadelphia Public Store distributed woolen single and double caps to the Virginia Line in the winter of 1778-1779 (PPS 1778-1779:9-25). These were probably knitted stocking caps. The double cap was a tube that tapered to both ends and then one end was inserted into the other providing a double thickness of material (Hanson 1981:11).

GAITERS

Gaiters were part of the first uniform of the Virginian troops and probably used throughout the war. They were made from thick woolen cloth and heavy linen. There were two types of gaiters: full gaiters and half gaiters or spatterdashes. The full gaiters extended above the knee and the half gaiters above the ankle to approximately the bottom of the calf.

Both types of gaiters buttoned their full length on the outside of the leg. They had a tongue of material inserted at the front to cover the front of the shoe. A strap attached to each side at the bottom ran under the arch of the shoe. The full gaiters were bound below the knee with a garter, usually a leather strap with a buckle. Possibly a strip of cloth might be used for this purpose. Although the gaiter is often compared to the leggings worn by Native Americans, the garment was common to the European soldier of the period and was probably used by civilians whose work would cause unusual wear on breeches, stockings, and shoes.

SHOES

The lack of shoes was a continuous problem for the Continental Army. Obviously, this item of equipment would have received the most wear. The problem was one of quality as well as quantity and is summed up in this statement by General Washington on March 6, 1778:

> ... we have suffered more for want of shoes than for any other article (and those imported from France afford little more than a days wear) (WGW 11, 1934:35).

The problem had not improved since the previous fall. The following quote from General Weedon would suggest the problem was especially difficult and little was expected from the states.

The Commander in Chief offers a $10 reward for the person who produces the best substitute for shoes out of raw hides (Weedon 1971:138).

The soldier's shoe was the common shoe of the period. Produced on straight lasts it could be worn on either foot. It may have had a square or rounded toe. Although it could be modified to tie with laces, a buckle closure was common (Neumann and Kravic 1975:122-123). Shoe buckles were issued to the Virginians in 1778-1779 (PPS 1778-1779:14-16).

REGIMENTAL COAT (Figures 2 & 3)

There is no known example of an American enlisted man's coat. Models are constructed from English coats, period illustrations, and coats of American officers. As the deserter descriptions have shown, Virginians used a variety of coats, civilian and military. The model described is based on military regulations and probably was available to the Virginia Line from 1778 to the close of the war.

The Virginian's coat was standardized along with the rest of the Army in a general order issued on October 2, 1779. Each state's line regiments were to conform to a program calling for blue coats, faced with a specific color. Virginia, along with Pennsylvania, Delaware, and Maryland, was to use red facings. All infantry coats were to have white linings and white buttons (Goodwin 1962:x).

The coat was constructed to fit close to the body. It came to about mid-thigh. The body of the coat was wool broadcloth; the facings, cuffs, and collar were perhaps of a different wool material. The buttons, cast in white metal, were used on each facing, the cuffs, and in back at the top of the vents. They may have been plain or the continental buttons with the letters USA in relief. The coat had pocket flaps on each side.

The collar of the coat turned down. The coat closed in front from the collar to mid chest with hooks and eyes. In cold weather a facing could be unbuttoned, folded across, and buttoned on top of the other facing. Also the cuffs could be unbuttoned and turned down in cold weather. The tails on each side of the coat were turned back and fastened with a hook and eye reinforced by a small heart shape piece of material sewn on the lining. These could be let down in cold weather (Klinger 1967:13-15).

The French supplied coats to the Americans and these may have been issued in the winter of 1778-1779 (Mollo 1975:204). They came in two colors: brown and blue, both faced with red. The blue coats were preferred, so a lottery was held to decide which state's line regiments would get which color. The Virginia Line probably received these lottery coats in brown and blue. Virginia was shipping uniforms north just when the French supplies were available. It is difficult to determine what the Virginia soldiers had in the autumn of 1778, or later.

FIREARMS

The American Revolution, 1775-1883, is within the era of military firearms dominated by the smoothbore flintlock musket. The period of the flintlock extends from the late seventeenth century to the 1840's and, due to an arms shortage, some saw service in the early days of the American Civil War. The flintlock smoothbore musket gradually replaced the matchlock and edged weapons, such as the pike or polearm, as the standard infantry weapon and remained dominant until it was replaced by the caplock rifled musket.

Flintlock ignition systems were developed c.1550 and, for the next century and a half, competed with the matchlock and wheel-lock systems. The matchlock, which replaced the longbow and crossbow in warfare, was by comparison to the other two ignition systems slow to fire, bulky in size, and undependable in bad weather. The wheel-lock fired faster than a matchlock and was far more dependable. It rivaled the flintlock in this regard. However, it was a more complicated mechanism and required precision in manufacture and maintenance.

The flintlock saw distinct stages in its development but by the middle of the seventeenth century it had achieved the form that is found on the muskets of the American Revolution. Its function was the same as the other systems, to ignite a quantity of gunpowder that would propel a projectile. This was accomplished by loading the barrel of the firearm with a measured amount of gunpowder followed by a round lead ball that may be wrapped in cloth, leather, or paper to seal the area between the ball and the barrel wall. The ball and its wadding would be pressed tight against the powder charge with the ramrod.

The flintlock ignition system is mounted on the side of the firearm at the breech end of the barrel with the lock's pan in line with a small opening in the barrel called a touch hole, or vent, that exposes the powder charge. A small quantity of gunpowder, the priming, is put into the pan of the lock. When the trigger is pulled the cock is released, and driven by a compressed spring, the flint strikes the frizzen. The flint scrapes particles of metal, heated by the friction, from the frizzen, while throwing the frizzen forward exposing the priming powder. This shower of sparks ignites the powder in the pan, the flash travels through the vent igniting the main powder charge discharging the weapon. Given good design, craftsmanship in manufacture, and no more than a moderate amount of moisture in the air, this process, from trigger pull to discharge, will appear instantaneous.

The failure of the weapon to fire in the hands of a colonist hunting duck or deer may have been inconvenient. The failure to fire in the hands of a soldier may have been fatal, for himself and his comrades. Where the colonist may have had his weapon produced by a local craftsman, whose livelihood depended on the quality of his product, the soldier's weapon may have been produced under a government contract motivated by a critical need. Cost control, for the contractor, dominated the production of the military weapon and reputation of the producer was of less consequence, than that of a local craftsman. Military weapons had a reputation for indifferent quality.

Potential problems of the military musket were offset by an additional piece of equipment and appropriate tactics employed by the armies of the period. Military muskets were fitted with a bayonet to make it useful when it failed to operate for whatever reason, or the enemy was too close to allow reloading. The bayonet was first introduced in a plug type. This was a metal blade with a round wood handle forced into the muzzle of the musket's barrel. This had two problems. The bayonet had to be removed if the musket was to be loaded and fired. Also, the bond between musket and bayonet was not sound. Movement of the musket or using the bayonet would affect its attachment to the musket.

An improvement was made by the introduction of the socket type bayonet. This bayonet connected the blade to a metal tube with a short piece of metal, the neck. The tube slipped over the muzzle of the barrel and was secured by the groove in the tube engaging a metal lug welded to the barrel. The blade would then be parallel to the barrel but offset. This arrangement allowed the musket to be loaded and fired without removing the bayonet. The socket bayonet was the type that saw service in the Revolution. Civilian arms were pressed into service early in the war and, due to these arms lacking a bayonet lug, the plug bayonet may have been used. It would easily adapt to these arms. Also, the rifle, which most often had an octagonal shape to the exterior of the barrel, would not accept a socket bayonet. The plug bayonet may have been used to offset this deficiency.

Battle tactics of the Revolution, called linear, were designed to take best advantage of the characteristics of the military musket. Opposing forces lined up facing each other in ranks two or three deep and fired in the general direction of the opponent. Muskets may have had the range to send a ball 200 yards but it generally could not consistently hit a man at more than 80 yards. They were not provided with the rear sight that is necessary for accuracy in aiming the weapon. Rather than drilling the soldier in shooting accurately, the soldier was drilled in speed of loading. The quantity of fire rather than the quality, and the courage to engage with the bayonet, was considered the measure of a good army.

Tactics dictated by the limitations of the flintlock muskets revolved around an attempt to bring a superior force, in numbers, against an inferior opponent. This equation will, of course, be modified by the ability, experience, and morale of the combatants. The advantage, due to these military qualities, went to the British forces early in the war. However, the Americans began to show an ability to hold their own as the war went on.

As with every other commodity, supplying firearms to the soldiers was a major problem. French assistance eased the problem in 1777. Yet, for the first two years of the war procurement of suitable weapons was, for Virginia, a make-do proposition.

There were four sources of supply available to the state. Some volunteers brought a personal weapon with them. There were weapons captured in armories and in early battles. Also,

Virginia, like other states, contracted with local craftsmen to produce weapons in quantity and encouraged a fledgling weapons industry. Finally, the state attempted to purchase firearms in Europe (Goodwin 1962:162. Neumann 1967:22).

All these sources supplied weapons for the Virginia soldier. Although the results may have met the initial problem of supplying the soldier with a firearm, the variety of weapons caused a supply nightmare. Ammunition supply had to service barrel bore diameters that ranged between .65 and .80 inches in muskets and the low end of the range increases when rifles are added. Although a musket can accommodate a wider tolerance between bore and ball size than a rifle, and therefore is forgiving if strict specifications are not met, the army quartermaster had a problem. Also, spare parts were needed from time to time. Interchangeable parts were, of course, not available. To fit a part on a flintlock the armorer first had to have a part that approximated the part to be replaced, then he would have to modify it for the particular weapon. The supplies had to include parts for British, Dutch, German, and locally produced weapons.

Colonial militia custom, if not law, required that every man provide his own equipment, this included a firearm. It can be assumed that many personal arms were brought to the regimental camps at the beginning of the war. These personal weapons were for hunting, although they may have served a self-defense role in the western Virginia counties and for Virginians who were exploring further west. Many soldiers living in the western counties favored rifles rather than smoothbore weapons, this weapon will be discussed later.

These personal weapons presented a variety of types. Long-barrelled fowling guns, or fowlers, designed to be loaded with shot for duck or goose hunting, were probably found among the men from tidewater counties. Locally produced arms, with a mixture of colonial-produced and European parts, might be found in any part of the state, as might obsolete military muskets and economically produced weapons for the Indian trade. A well-to-do gentleman would provide his own fusil, a proportionally smaller version of a military musket mounted with silver or other fine metal decoration.

Many men enlisted with no equipment. The state encouraged the establishment of a factory at Fredericksburg and contracted with individuals to produce muskets (Goodwin 1962:162). Gunsmithing is a skilled and labor-intensive endeavor, and the needs of the colonial civilian population cannot compare with the emergency military need at the beginning of the war. The records are sketchy about how well local production met demand, however, there were not enough skilled individuals to produce a small fraction of the need. The only firearm supply that could address the need of Virginia and the rest of the states was where firearm manufacturing had been an ongoing activity, in Europe.

Of course, Virginia was not alone in the need for firearms. Other states in the Continental Congress, like Virginia, had agents competing in Europe for guns. There was some success, as the *Virginia Gazette*, August 9 and November 20, 1776, recorded the arrival of two shipments. These references unfortunately do not state the origin of the muskets. A secondary source, however, provides an undated reference to 2100 firearms reaching Williamsburg from Rotterdam (Brown 1980:320). This may suggest purchase of Dutch firearms by the state, although the low countries were regular shipping points for products from other parts of inland Europe.

DOCUMENTARY EVIDENCE

A popular idea concerning the American soldiers in the Revolution is that they were poorly supplied and what they did have in the way of equipment was of questionable quality. This idea has myth qualities; the ragtag Continental facing the well-equipped British professional. There is, like all myths, some truth to this view. The British soldier was, at most times, better supplied, although the quality of his equipment, including firearms, was only comparable to the Americans. He was a better soldier than the American at the beginning of the war, judged by European standards and the practice of military science in the eighteenth century.

At the outset of the war the Americans, Virginians included, faced shortages of all war materials. As discussed throughout this study, Virginia used whatever was at hand to supply troops into the field. This is especially true of firearms. The qualities of the standard military muskets are discussed above, as are general sources of supply. Now specific references to firearms will be examined to learn what sort of firearm was used by the soldier of the Virginia Continental Line.

The state's need was met in several ways. As mentioned earlier, many men brought their own weapons, especially the men from the west where a firearm was an important survival tool. The need for a firearm in the settled east was less, and there were new immigrants and young men who did not have the financial ability to provide themselves with a musket.

Virginians captured a few weapons at the Battle of Great Bridge in December 1775. Among the captured arms retained for the army by Colonel Woodford were thirty "well fixed" muskets and two silver mounted fuzees (VG, December 16, 1775). The muskets might have been either the English manufactured Long Land or Short Land pattern, both were being used by the British Army at this time. The fuzees (fusils) were a shorter, lighter version of the military musket. The silver mountings mark these as officers' weapons, made by independent contractors to government specifications.

Virginians were also involved in the Christmas Day attack on the German troops garrisoning Trenton, New Jersey. At this engagement one thousand muskets were captured (Smith 1976:822). It seems reasonable that deficiencies in arms among Washington's soldiers were made up from these stores. This may have included Virginians.

Virginia also looked to arms produced in the colonies. The Committee of Safety, by law, had full power to purchase weapons in other colonies (Goodwin 1962:162). Between September 1775, and July 1776, the Virginia Committee of Safety purchased 3325 muskets and 2098 rifles (Gill 1974:34). Pennsylvania and Massachusetts produced some of the largest numbers of arms. Pennsylvania contractors received orders for forty-five hundred stands of arms between October 1, 1775 and April 30, 1776 (Brown 1980:309).

Contracts were also made within Virginia. On September 28, 1776, 200 stands of arms were ordered from the Hunter Iron Works, previously known as Rappahannock Forge, in Falmouth, Virginia. There were a few other works around the state. The record of production by Virginia's gun makers is unclear. However, there was a continuing demand and they did supply what they could. Hunter's and the Virginia State Factory, at the junction of the James and Rivanna Rivers, were still operating until the invasions of 1780-1781. Virginia established a new arsenal at Point of Forks in 1783, which operated until 1803 (Brown 1980:313).

These multiple sources of arms seem to have been sufficient to allow Virginians to take the field with Washington. Although they had weapons, problems with the supply of suitable ammunition and spare parts, as mentioned earlier, continued. The situation is illustrated by an order issued by a Virginia Regiment:

June 25, 1776

The Capts. in command of each company are desired instantly to give in an exact account of their arms and accoutrements, whether they be musquets or common small guns, the number of rifles fit or unfit for duty, how they are fixed for molds, and c.; in short to give as an exact account as possible of the weakness of our regiment (Stubblefield 1887:186-187).

The most interesting word in this order is weakness. This does not necessarily mean shortage. The weakness in Stubblefield's opinion might be the mix of weapons and the condition. He refers to muskets, common guns (civilian weapons), and rifles. The characteristics of these weapons are discussed in this chapter's introduction. This officer and his peers were becoming more proficient with the standard linear tactics, at least in drill. These tactics called for reliance on the musket with the bayonet. Common guns and rifles did not have the capacity to mount a bayonet. Consequently, if facing an equal number of the enemy, Stubblefield's command might have held their own in a shooting battle. They might have been superior, if the tactics were limited to firing, considering they had rifles. If, however, the battle was to be decided in the accepted fashion, the bayonet charge, the Virginians were weak indeed.

This situation was not limited to one regiment. In October 1776, General Stephen requested muskets to replace rifles in the 4th Virginia Regiment (Sanchez-Saavedra 1978:42). Another regiment, the 11th Virginia, was commanded by Daniel Morgan who led the first Virginians, riflemen, north to Boston in 1775. There were, undoubtedly, many rifles in his command.

In 1777, Washington had formed a Corps of Riflemen, under the command of Morgan. This was an attempt to use the rifles in a role that suited their characteristics, long range shooting with accuracy, but with the protection of line troops when threatened with enemy bayonets. Unfortunately, the problem of mixed firearms in the line regiments plagued Morgan at the beginning.

> 13 June 1777
> Rifles are to be given to Morgan's corps for muskets
> if not enough they are to exchange or purchase private
> property (Heth 1892:357).

It can be assumed that the problems confronting the regiments mentioned above were shared by other Virginia units. A noticeable improvement occurred when a large quantity of imported French muskets reached the army.

When the Virginia Line surrendered with the Charleston garrison in May 1780, it gave up its arms. British records show that fifty-five hundred men surrendered 5416 French muskets (Taliaferro 1980:34-35). It must be concluded that at this point in time the Virginians were armed in large part, if not completely, with French muskets. The problem remains to figure out when they first received these arms.

France was the major supplier of muskets for the Americans. It is estimated that 102,000 muskets were received from France between 1776 and 1781. Although the quantity is large the quality may be questioned, if for no other reason than the French probably sent a variety of models of their obsolete military muskets. There were possibly seven different models shipped: M1717, M1728, M1746, M1754, M1763, M1766, and M1768 (Butler 1971:27-28). These model numbers indicate the year in which a particular design was accepted, although individual arms might not have conformed to the standard pattern. The mixture of models and the differences in quality is reflected in a letter from General Nathanael Greene to George Washington:

> A Brigg arrived this day from Nantz [Nantes]. Her cargo consists of 272 Chests of arms containing 6800, sixty chests of which not being fully proved, the Capt. says he cannot so fully engage for their goodness, but the remaining 212 chests are very fine proved arms. Also, 1500 excellent double bridled locks (Greene 2, 1980:48).

Besides being a division and later a department commander, Greene served for a time as quartermaster general. Washington had great confidence in him and his record in each position is commendable. His opinion concerning these arms can be accepted with confidence. His reference to double-bridled locks and very fine proved arms might suggest later model muskets, most likely M1763.

The French arms, after arrival, had to be delivered to the army and transportation difficulties caused some delay. Ships from France, or from an intermediate port such as St. Eustatius in the Caribbean, would naturally seek a port of least resistance from the British Navy. The British maintained a naval blockade of the American coast, attempting to intercept these supplies. The navy, however, had the added responsibility of supporting the army. Consequently, the majority of naval vessels were in waters near the conflicting armies: New York City, New Jersey, and eastern Pennsylvania. That the supply ships avoided these areas is supported by records of shipments to Portsmouth, New Hampshire, and Williamsburg, Virginia.

Portsmouth is the most frequently mentioned port of delivery. French muskets (41,680) were delivered here between October 1776, and December 1777 (Brown 1980:319). In March 1777, a vessel reached Portsmouth with 12,000 muskets and another 11,987 were delivered in April 1777 (WGW 7, 1932:216. Brown 1980:319). These two deliveries account for half the total received through this port.

Philadelphia was the closest port to the normal area of operations of Washington's army. Shipments arriving here would make delivery of the muskets and other supplies to the troops much easier. Reaching Philadelphia, however, would have been much more dangerous for the vessels, as Royal Navy activity would have been heavier on the mid-Atlantic coast. This activity was not only to intercept supplies for the colonists but also to protect the supplies for the British army from American privateers.

The risk seems to have been worthwhile. Between February 1776, and February 1779, a total of 14,156 muskets were delivered to Philadelphia (Brown 1980:319). Washington notes that 11,000 were in Philadelphia in March 1777 (WGW 7, 1932:216). The importance of this city as a supply port may have been one of the reasons for the British campaign in the fall 1777, to capture it, which they did, after defeating the Americans at the Battle of Brandywine. The British abandoned the city in the spring of 1778 and returned to New York City.

French and other European arms were not being shipped exclusively to northern ports. The *Virginia Gazette* periodically reports the arrival of arms and other supplies in nearby waters. On March 21, 1777, a ship arrived in the James River from Nantes with fifteen hundred stands of arms. Again on April 4 of the same year the brig *Sally* arrived with 10,000 stands of arms and gun locks. A French warship and two merchant vessels from Rochefort arrived on May 29, 1778, with arms and dry goods. There were, undoubtedly, other shipments direct from Europe, from Europe via the Caribbean, and from the activity of privateers.

The abundance of good harbors and an intercoastal waterway on the Atlantic coast produced an active water-based shipping trade early in American history. This was to the detriment of a road system. Unfortunately, during the Revolution the waterways, as mentioned above, were the domains of the Royal Navy. This made overland shipment of arms and other supplies necessary. Transportation may have been the major reason for lack of supply to the army rather than inept administrators and inefficient contractors.

The potential transportation problem can be illustrated by considering the movement of muskets from the coast to the army. References of numbers of chests of arms to total arms place the number of muskets per chest between twenty-five and thirty-two. If the smaller number is used and the weight of a musket is 10 pounds then, with the weight of a stout wood container, each chest would be more than 250 pounds. A conservative estimate of the size of each chest (62" by 18" by 18") would allow perhaps twelve chests per wagon. Whereas a wagon could support one and one-half tons, a problem arises when the quality of colonial roads is considered. It is perhaps more realistic to consider a wagon load at half the size or six chests or 150 muskets. This would supply one, understrength, regiment.

The arms shipments from France peaked in early 1777. This abundance seems to have reached the Virginia Line late in the summer of that year. An order was issued by General George Weedon in August 1777, to his brigade of Virginia Line to return chests for extra arms. This suggests that arms had been issued recently, and the need for extra arms suggests that present needs had been filled (Weedon 1971:26). The date of Weedon's order strongly suggests that his brigade received French muskets. To simplify ammunition supply, the army made an effort to maintain a uniformity of firearms within related army units. Consequently, it is probable that the other Virginia brigades received French muskets. Washington issued orders to have each brigade or division be armed with weapons of the same size bore, "as many happy consequences would flow from it" (WGW 9, 1933:363).

The winter of 1777-1778, was hard on firearms and the soldiers. In May 1778, Washington requested that the Commissary of Military Stores in Springfield, Massachusetts, send two thousand arms, as "The distress of this Army for want of arms is very great." A postscript requests, "Let 1000 more arms be packed up, to be sent on, on orders being given" (WGW 11, 1934:409).

The next day Washington wrote to the President of Congress:

> I think the Arms and Clothing expected from France, should be brought forward without a moments delay after they arrive.... Our distress is amazingly great. We have many men without firelocks, and many coming in, in the same predicament (WGW 11, 1934,416).

Obviously, new recruitment was causing part of the supply shortage. This and other related problems were apparently solved, as there is no mention of similar problems in Washington's writings or other records. The problems of late 1778, and early 1779, centered on clothing. There is little reference to arms shortages in the Virginia Line until the surrender at Charleston in 1780.

Virginia's war effort, after the loss of the state's regiments at Charleston, faced many problems. Perhaps the greatest problem was that the war had come to Virginia's soil. British troops raided supply locations, destroyed factories, and chased the government for much of 1780 and 1781. During this period Virginia attempted to recruit replacement troops, supply them, and supply continental army detachments under Von Steuben and Lafayette who had been sent south to do what they could against the British. Besides defending herself, Virginia was asked to furnish men to the small army in the South under General Horatio Gates and later Nathanael Greene.

The problems facing Virginia's "government on the run," also resulted in limited records. Those that are available show that arms supplies became short during this period. Before the invasion of 1780-1781, there was a good supply of arms in the state. The Virginia Board of War reported on August 28, 1779, that 5000 imported stands of arms had been retained in Virginia (PTJ 3, 1951:78). In January 1781, the picture had changed. Jefferson's papers show that the supply in magazines had dwindled to 68 stands of arms (PTJ 4, 1951:470-471).

As was the case early in the war, supply of arms amounted to make do with what was available. In March 1782, William Davies, who late in the war commanded Virginia's military effort, wrote to the governor requesting that General Von Steuben be required to return the arms furnished him when he was operating in Virginia in 1780-1781 (CVSP 3, 1968:86). He suggests that these be replaced with those captured at Yorktown in 1781. These arms were, of course, British, and having a different bore size would have brought on the old problem of ammunition supply. Fortunately for the Virginians, this was late in the conflict and had no critical effect.

The firearms used by the Virginia soldier can be divided into three periods. The middle period, that of uniformity, 1777-1780, due to French supply is found between two periods of making do with what was at hand. The greatest variety of arms is found at the beginning of the war. The problems connected with this variety of arms, and the solving of these problems by the availability of the French musket, greatly affected Virginia and the nation.

MUSKETS

The documentary evidence strongly suggests that the soldier of the Virginia Continental Line carried an imported French musket from the summer of 1777 until the surrender at Charleston in 1780. Therefore, this part of the study will concentrate on the French musket. The English musket and American muskets, which were used by Virginians, will be discussed for comparative purposes.

All military muskets used in the American Revolution were essentially the same. They were, by modern standards, long and heavy. They were fired by means of a flintlock ignition system, the barrels were smoothbore, and they loaded from the muzzle. There were minor changes to the military musket throughout the eighteenth century. The changes may have had some effect on reliability, operation, and maintenance. They could not, however, be thought of as evolutionary in firearm technology.

The French musket saw many more changes than the British arm. Authorities recognize two models of British muskets during a period in which there are nine models of French muskets (Neumann 1967:34-35). Although any or all of these French models may have been part of those supplied to the Continental Army, it is believed the bulk of those imported were models of 1763, 1766, and 1768 (Peterson 1968:38, Neumann 1967:35).

The model 1763 will serve as an example of the French musket. It must be noted that individual specimens may or may not be true to the ideal. Repairs may have included parts from other models altered to fit or parts manufactured by army artificers or civilian gunsmiths. Repairs or personal modifications may have changed a musket substantially from original specifications.

The M1763 musket (Figure 4a) had a 44 1/2-inch barrel with a 69-caliber bore. It was held to the wooden stock with three metal bands. The lock had a flat cock and lockplate 6 3/4 inches long. The barrel bands, lock, and other metal parts were iron. One example of the M1763 musket is 59 3/4 inches overall. The lock measures 6 3/4 inches by 1 3/4 inches. The trigger guard is 12 5/8 inches and the butt tang, 2 1/2 inches. It weighs 9.3 lbs. This musket has CHARLEVILLE engraved and US stamped or engraved on the lock plate (Neumann 1967:72). Charleville was one of the three French armories. The others were Maubeuge and St. Etienne. The author of this study has seen only one musket marked St. Etienne and many marked Charleville. Charleville has become a common name for any French musket of the Revolutionary War. The US marking establishes the musket as property of the United States. Sling swivels were mounted on lugs on the middle barrel band and in front of the bow of the trigger guard. A sight was fixed on the front barrel band. The ramrod was iron (Neumann 1967:72).

The musket carried by the British soldier, and some Americans, was functionally identical to the French. There are, however, differences that are readily visible. These differences

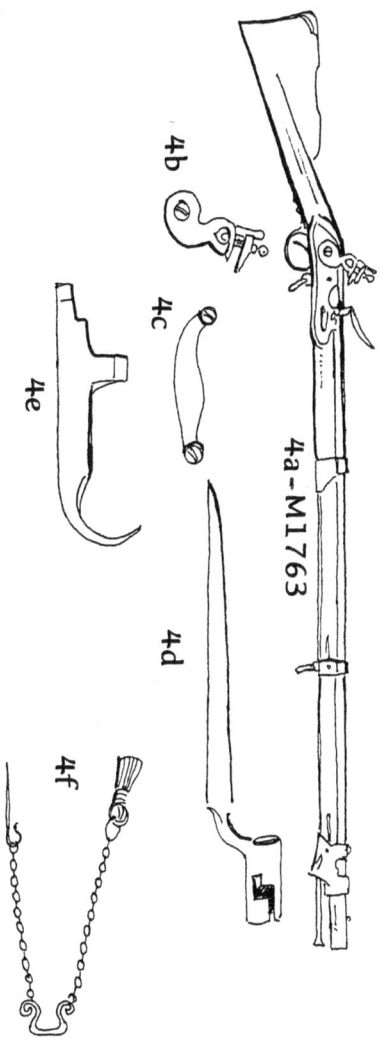

4b

4c

4e

4a – M1763

4d

4f

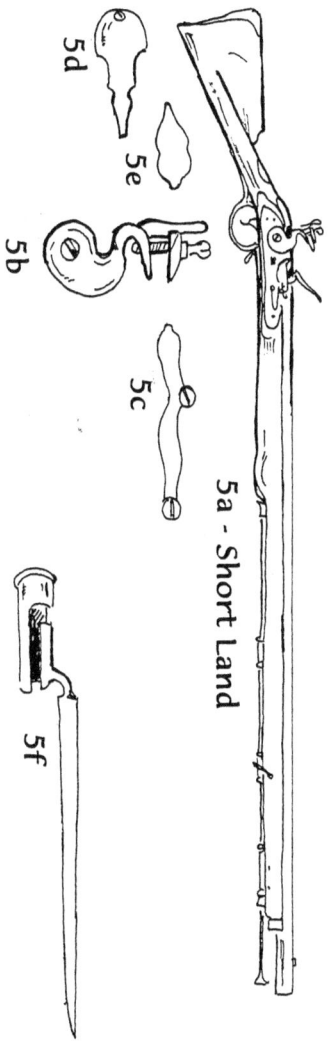

5d

5e

5b

5c

5a – Short Land

5f

Joe Lee
96

may have affected individual perceptions of the musket's quality. The English military musket is commonly known as the Brown Bess, although it is questioned as to whether this term was used before or during the war (Brown 1980:231). There are two models of the Bess used by the British army during the American Revolution: the Long Land pattern or first model, and the Short Land pattern or second model.

The Long Land pattern appeared in the early 1720's. It had a 46-inch barrel which was attached to the wooden stock with metal pins. The pins passed through the stock and engaged lugs on the bottom of the barrel. The earliest muskets had iron furniture, a holdover from the earlier Queen Anne muskets. Brass replaced iron as the latter was used up. By 1730, brass was the standard (Neumann 1967:33).

A 42-inch barrel, the main characteristic of the Short Land pattern musket (Figure 5a), appeared in 1722, although it was not officially accepted until the 1740's. The Short Land pattern was formally adopted in 1768. The Long Land pattern, however, continued to be produced until 1790 (Neumann 1967:33-34).

Differences between the French and English muskets included the pinning of the barrel on the English weapon. This required that more wood be left in the stock than was the case with the banding technique on the French gun. This accounted in part for the English arm being heavier than the French. The French M1763, previously noted, weighed 9.3 lbs. This is a heavy example. Other muskets, including an M1754, M1746-1763, M1766, and M1768, weighed 8.5, 8.8, 8.0, and 8.4 lbs. respectively. Examples of English muskets weighed between 9.4 and 10.5 lbs. for the Long Land pattern, and 10.0 to 10.8 lbs. for the Short Land pattern (Neumann 1967:58-62, 70-74). Weight is a characteristic that would be readily noticeable and important to the soldier. Many soldiers in the Continental Army, Virginians included, had experience with both weapons (Peterson 1968:27, 36-38). This experience was to contribute to the selection and production of American military arms in the future.

It might also be assumed that the iron furniture of the French arm was preferred to the brass found on the English gun. The day-to-day maintenance of the musket in the field was the responsibility of the soldier. This included the cleaning of the metal parts. Both iron and brass are susceptible to surface corrosion. The shine of brass, that would suggest a well maintained arm is not possible on iron. Therefore, the soldier with an iron mounted gun would not have to produce the very visible results required of a brass mounted gun.

American-produced muskets resembled the English models. This was, undoubtedly, a result of tradition and the availability of parts scavenged from obsolete and broken muskets. There may have been many of these muskets in local magazines, surplus from the French and Indian War or earlier conflicts. Although the American product resembles its English counterpart, there are significant differences.

A small sample of seven American-made muskets attributed to the period 1775-1783, support the points stated above. Five of the examples have bore diameters smaller than the English muskets whose bore was approximately .75 caliber. Four of these muskets are .71-.74 caliber and one is .67. The musket with the .67 caliber bore is closer to the bore size of a French musket than an English. This weapon also has a French style side plate and butt plate, which, like the rest of the furniture, are brass. It is lighter, 9.3 lbs., than the other examples that range up to 11.0 lbs. The lock is an English style. This musket, although thought to be manufactured during the Revolution, is marked "6 V. SPOTSYLVANIA", a marking system attributed to the 1790's (Neumann 1967:108-112).

The reasons for the differences in these weapons from the English arms, which provided the pattern, might be just a case of working with the available resources. However, the smaller bore size would have allowed for economy in the amount of lead used in ammunition. This economy is thought to have been important to the gunsmiths of Pennsylvania (see Rifles below). Perhaps it was a reflection of a break with tradition.

RIFLES

It is clear from the documentation that early in the war many Virginia soldiers, including those in line regiments, were armed with rifles. There is no evidence to suggest when and if rifles were issued in any quantity to these men, therefore, the weapons were probably personal property. (Note: As mentioned earlier, Virginia did purchase rifles.) There was no standard model as with the muskets. This weapon would have been produced in the region of the soldier's home, and regional traditions were distinctive. Consequently, a variety of rifles would have been seen in the Virginia Continental Line.

The variety of rifles was due to Virginia being geographically between two regional traditions in gun making. These traditions, Pennsylvania and Southern, or Southern Mountain, exhibit very different characteristics in their product. Virginians would have been exposed to one or both styles.

The Pennsylvania rifles have been well documented as a combination of the gun making traditions of Central Europe, brought to Pennsylvania in the early eighteenth century by German immigrants, and the adaptation to the environment of North America. The rifle in Europe, commonly known as the jaeger, was a short, heavy weapon with a 28-inch barrel of .60 to .70 caliber. The thick wood stock had a patchbox with a sliding wood cover. The furniture was brass (Neumann 1967:134).

By the time of the American Revolution, this tradition, as practiced in Pennsylvania, had produced a very different variation of this weapon. For greater accuracy, the short barrel had been lengthened (to consume all the powder charge and provide a longer aiming span); for economy of lead and lighter weight, the bore was reduced; for a flatter trajectory, a higher ratio of powder to ball evolved; and for better balance in carrying through rough country, the stock was reshaped. By 1770, the American rifle destined for use in the Revolutionary War had acquired many of its basic characteristics: a barrel length over 40 inches; a bore averaging .40 to .60 caliber (with seven or eight grooves); a long thin stock extending to the muzzle; a gooseneck cock; an elevated handgrip on the rear of the triggerguard; raised carving around the fittings; and a patchbox with a wooden, iron, or simple brass cover (Neumann 1967:134).

An example of this type of weapon was used by Nicholas Allen of Virginia who served under Daniel Morgan. The sideplate is engraved "NA 1770". The builder is thought to be Jacobus Scout, a Pennsylvania gunsmith. The furniture is brass and the patchbox appears hinged on the bottom. Its overall length is 4 feet 11 inches (Moore 1967:177).

The Southern rifle is quite different. Although it shares basic characteristics, length and profile shape, it lacks the refinements of the Pennsylvania gun. There is little, if any, decorative carving, and when found it is usually only on the cheek piece. The furniture is iron and these parts were limited to a buttplate and ramrod pipes, with the rear ramrod pipe often omitted. A simple grease hole was drilled or cut into the stock in place of a patchbox. This held a thick lubricant to moisten patches.

An example of this type of weapon, with some interesting variations, is attributed to a Virginia gunsmith active before and during the war. The rifle, marked "M. SHEETS" on the barrel, is 64 3/4 inches overall with a 49- inch, .55 caliber, octagonal to round barrel. The stock has no cheekpiece, grease hole, or any other carving. This gun has brass furniture, not usual on a Southern rifle, although it conforms with the simple style of these weapons and does not have an elevated handgrip on the trigger guard (Neumann 1967:146).

Virginia bordered both the Pennsylvania and southern gun making traditions. The rifle carried by the Virginia soldier was probably purchased near his home and was of the style of that region. The Nicholas Allen rifle, described above, would support this contention. Many of Morgan's men came from the area of his home near Winchester, Virginia. This northern Virginia location would have made Pennsylvania rifles accessible to the local market.

ACCOUTREMENTS

CARTRIDGE BOXES, SHOT POUCHES

The containers for ammunition most familiar to the American colonists were the powder horn, or powder flask, and the shot pouch. Their weapon, rifle or musket, was loaded by pouring powder from the horn into a measure, the measure was then emptied into the barrel of the weapon, and the powder was followed by a ball or shot. The ball would be wrapped in a patch, a piece of cloth, which would fill the space between the ball and the barrel wall. This provided a gas seal and held the ball in the barrel. If shot was used it would be secured between wads. No matter which projectile used, it was seated firmly upon the powder charge using the ramrod. The amount of powder, type of patch or wadding, and type and sizes of projectile were dependent on the individual weapon and the task to be performed.

The ammunition containers used by the soldiers of the Continental Line were different. The soldier was supplied with cartridges, which were basically paper tubes sealed at both ends, which contained the powder and ball, with the paper wrapper providing the wadding. The soldier had to rip the cartridge open with his teeth, pour a small amount of the powder into the priming pan on the lock, pour the remainder of the powder into the musket's barrel, and ram the ball, with the cartridge paper, on top of the powder charge. This loading system was faster than the method employed by a hunter, as described above. Yet, the desire for speed in loading had a negative affect on the accuracy of the weapon. The paper, while it held the ball in place, made a poor gas seal. Add the lack of accuracy of the smoothbore musket and it is obvious why the tactics of the period were designed to emphasize rate of fire rather than accuracy. The hunter turned soldier surely would have viewed this as a waste of ammunition, an expensive commodity.

Another drawback to paper cartridges were their susceptibility to dampness. The paper provided only minimal protection to the powder and damp powder was useless. To solve this problem the soldier carried his ammunition in a leather cartridge box. Its design was based on two functional requirements; to protect the cartridges from the environment and allow easy access to the ammunition to maintain speed in loading the musket.

The requirements for the cartridge box allowed for some variety, but a quality box would feature some standard attributes. The box was a rectangular leather pouch, cut and sewn to accommodate a wood block. The block had holes drilled in it to hold individual paper cartridges. There was a thin leather flap, one edge of which was sewn to the body of the box in a way to allow the flap to lie on the top of the cartridge block. There was an outer flap that extended over the ends of the box and across the face of the box. This flap could be secured by a tab attached to the flap that could be fixed to a button on the bottom of the box. The outer flap was shaped so that, even when not fastened, it would remain closed.

At the beginning of the war many Virginians were armed with rifles and the paper cartridge system was unsuitable for this weapon. After the Virginia regiments joined the Continental Line the rifles were replaced with muskets. The documentation and examples that will be reviewed show that, while the Virginians of the Continental Line did use a cartridge box, the exact type used is open to speculation. Apparently the well-constructed box, described above, was rare.

The Virginians mustering at Williamsburg in 1775, found few, if any, military cartridge boxes in the colony's stores. The soldiers of the first regiments provided, or were supplied with, the familiar powderhorn and shot pouch. Although horns are not mentioned in the Williamsburg Public Store Record, it can be assumed they were used, as the companion shot pouches appear repeatedly in the early part of the record. Twill and duck, heavy canvas materials, were often issued for making shot pouches between October 12 and November 13, 1775 (Goodwin 1962:159-160). Whether this material was to make up deficiencies, as some men must have brought their own equipment, or if some companies were striving for uniformity is not clear.

The system soon began to change. An order for various items to William Lux and Company on December 13, 1775, included cartridge paper (Goodwin 1962:160). It is possible that pouches were used for paper cartridges, however, they would not provide the protection afforded by the leather cartridge boxes. Probably the Virginians used a variety of methods to keep their ammunition. An order issued on March 18, 1776, asks for the number of cartouch boxes, powderhorns, and shot pouches needed (Stubblefield 1887:155). The only mention of cartridge boxes in the Williamsburg Store is on April 10, 1777, is an entry for 200 cartouch boxes (Goodwin 1962:161). It would appear that the cartridge boxes used by the soldiers of the Virginia Line were supplied by the Continental Army.

The Continental Army also used a tin canister (Figure 6c) to carry ammunition. This was a simple rectangular container of tin-plated iron with a hinged lid whose edges fit over the body of the box. This provided a relatively waterproof container. The quality of this box is illustrated by an order of General Weedon noting the use of the tin ammunition canteens for other purposes (Weedon 1971:56). These other purposes are revealed in court action against Lt. Rains of the 15th Virginia. He sent a soldier to fetch water in a tin cartridge box (Weedon 1971:98).

The tin box had no divider and the cartridges were laid on top of one another. This would have not answered for the quick access to the ammunition provided by the leather cartridge box with each cartridge in an individual hole in the block. The tin box, although possibly used for the soldier's primary supply of ammunition, was probably designed for an auxiliary supply. An extra supply of ammunition would be especially important to troops on detached service away from the army's regular supply system. On July 25, 1779, Washington ordered that ammunition canisters be delivered to the Light Infantry (WGW 15, 1936:476). During the 1779 campaign, the Brigade of Light Infantry operated independently. Virginians made up a large part of the brigade.

FIGURE 6 - CARTRIDGE BOXES

6a

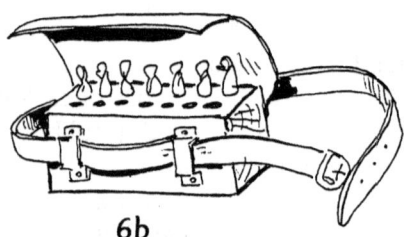

6b

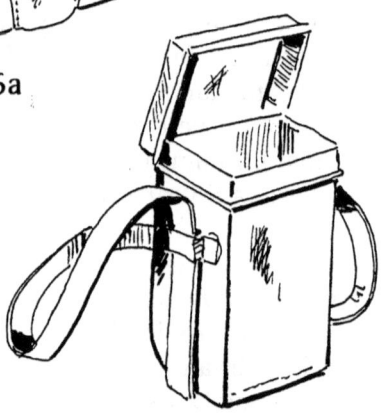

6c

Joe Lee
96

Virginians not part of the Light Infantry in 1779, also used the tin boxes. On September 1, 1777, Weedon ordered that 278 tin boxes for extra cartridges be divided between Muhlenberg's and Weedon's brigades (Weedon 1971:27). On September 25, 1777, Weedon ordered that the men were to carry only their cartridge boxes and tin canisters full (Weedon 1971:60). This suggests that the soldiers may have carried cartridges in their haversacks. Having both types of boxes may not have been the norm throughout the Army. An order from Washington on October 13, 1777, calls for tin canisters to be taken away from men with cartridge boxes to supply the men with neither item (WGW 9, 1933:363).

The men with the tin boxes may have been reluctant to give them up. They provided a reasonable assurance of usable ammunition. The quality of the leather boxes was always suspect. Timothy Pickering the Adjutant General of the Army remarked on this problem in September of 1777:

> Having been under arms nearly all day during an incessant rain, the ammunition and the cartridge boxes (which are badly made) was spoiled. This obliged us to keep out of striking distance but as near to the enemy as was compatible with that object until the army could safely encamp and make up musket cartridges. This occasioned two or three night marches (Wright 1963:69).

Washington was probably reacting to the same concern when he wrote to the Board of War three months earlier:

> Be pleased to send on all the Tin Cartridge Canisters and have as many more made as possible, they will save an immense amount of ammunition (WGW 8, 1933:272-273).

Washington's concern over the quality of the cartridge boxes continued, as is evident from the following letters. On October 13, 1777, he wrote to the President of Congress:

None but the best and thickest (leather)... small inner flap...the flaps in general, are too small and do not project sufficiently over the ends or the sides of the boxes (WGW 9, 1933:366).

To the Board of War, November 3, 1777:

Lining the flap with painted canvas will certainly be of service, considering the badness and thinness of the leather in general; but the greatest preservative to the cartridges, is a small inside flap of pliant leather, which lays close upon them and not only keeps them dry but from being rubbed (WGW 9, 1933:497).

The campaign of 1778 saw the quality of the cartridge boxes was secondary to the problem of availability. Again Washington writes to the Board of War, June 6, 1778:

...we are exceedingly distressed for Cartouch Boxes. By an exact return made a few days ago 1700 were wanting for the new recruits, and to replace ol ones,... (WGW 12, 1934:25).

Washington in a letter to General William Maxwell on August 13, 1778, states the situation clearly: "Commissary of Military Stores has no cartrouch boxes or tin canisters" (WGW 12, 1934:318).

It may be that necessity is the mother of invention or, perhaps, production. At least one factory in Philadelphia was turning out 60-70 boxes per day in the spring of 1779 (WGW 15, 1936:158). It seems that this rate of production and the general inactivity of the Army in 1779 would have contributed to the easing of concern connected to the availability of cartridge boxes.

The problem that remains is to understand what style of cartridge box, other than the tin canisters, was carried by soldiers of the Virginia Line. There is no description or other identification of any particular model. The only clue available from the documentation is the number of rounds issued to each soldier. Since the individual cartridge was susceptible to damage from various causes, it seems likely that the soldiers were only issued a quantity of ammunition that could be accommodated in the cartridge box.

A division order and general order issued by General Weedon on September 13, 1777, calls for each man to get 40 rounds and extra ammunition to be carried in such a way to prevent injury and loss (Weedon 1971:46, 48-49). Does the issue of 40 rounds correspond to the capacity of a box? Some men had tin canisters besides the leather box. The tin canisters had a capacity of 36 rounds. The wooden block in a leather box had from nine to thirty-six holes for cartridges (Neumann and Kravic 1975:66,67). It would appear the tin canisters were considered in orders for ammunition issues at this time. Yet, on January 26, 1778, Weedon again issues an order for 40 rounds to be issued to each man (Weedon 1971:209). This comes after an order on January 10, 1778 to return all tin canisters (Weedon 1971:189).

The Virginia soldier used a tin canister besides the regular leather cartridge box throughout much of the war. The canister, it appears, came in only one variety. The leather box may have been of local manufacture, a French import, or a captured British or German box. The box of the soldier probably changed through the war. The first boxes were simple militia boxes (Figure 6b) adequate for short periods of service. These may have been followed by captured boxes and French imports. Evidence suggests that later in the war Continental production supplied the need. It seems probable that, like clothing and other equipment, there may very well have been a mixture of cartridge box styles within a regiment.

Examples of tin canisters are a deep rectangular container measuring 6 1/2" by 3 3/4" by 2 7/8" (Figure 6b.). It has a hinged lid with edges turned down to fit close to the body of the canister, sealing it from the weather. The canister was slung from a shoulder strap that passed through 1 1/2" wide tin loops soldered to the sides. The canister held thirty-six cartridges in layers of four across (Neumann and Kravic 1975:67).

The cartridge box was simply a rectangular pouch that held a wooden block with cylindrical holes to hold individual paper cartridges. A leather flap was sewn to the back of the pouch, crossed over the top and front of the box and fastened on the bottom. This flap would be slightly wider than the box. A leather or linen strap allowed the box to be slung from the shoulder. The leather strap may have been two pieces with a buckle (Neumann and Kravic 1975:66-80).

Various refinements were made to the basic model described above. The end pieces of the body of the box were made higher to extend above the top of the block. These pieces were rounded on the top to conform with the bend of the flap as it closed over the box. Often a piece of thin leather was sewn to the back of the box inside the outer flap (Figure 6a.). This lay on the cartridges for added protection. Canvas (possibly pointed) may have substituted for the leather inner flap in some boxes.

Boxes used late in the war may have had tin trays under the blocks that held musket tools and/or extra flints. A small flap of leather on the front of the box covered an opening that allowed access to this tray without removing the block. These tools (Figure 4e) and flints were carried in small pouches attached to the front of the box (Neumann and Kravic 1975:76, 78).

BAYONETS

An order from the state of Virginia for 200 "stands of arms" specified that this included a bayonet (Goodwin 1962:162). The nature of eighteenth-century warfare would allow the assumption that military muskets, no matter the source, had a bayonet as part of a "stand of arms." There was not, it appears, a shortage of bayonets except in the winter/spring of 1778. Weedon complained of deficiencies of bayonets on January 17 (Weedon 1971:194). On March 20, Washington wrote to the Board of War concerning the problem but he also says that the army is manufacturing its own (WGW 11, 1934:112). Fabricating a bayonet would not be a problem for a blacksmith.

If shortages did occur, it may have not have been in the number of bayonets available in stores but rather a proper bayonet for a particular musket. As with other spare parts, one size did not fit all. Minor adjustments could easily be made by an army artificer.

Another reason for need may have resulted from breakage due to improper use. The bayonet was used as a screwdriver (Taliaferro 1980:74). It would certainly serve to hold a hunk of meat over a cook fire. The effect of this heating may have made the metal quite brittle and when the bayonet was used as a pry bar to open a box or barrel it could easily break.

The bayonet design was, like the musket, unique to its place of manufacture. Therefore, if the musket used by the Virginia soldier can be identified, the bayonet style will also be identified. Probably, there were locally made replacements for lost or broken bayonets used on imported muskets. This diversity is probably no greater for bayonets than any other piece of equipment. As the French model 1763 musket has been used as the example of the firearm used by the Virginia soldier, it is appropriate to use the M1763 bayonet (Figure 4d) in the same role. It was slightly over seventeen inches long overall including a blade of about fourteen inches. This model introduced a locking ring that was rotated after the bayonet was fixed to the musket. This prevented the bayonet from slipping from the musket's barrel.

OTHER EQUIPMENT

The soldiers of the Virginia line regiments had access to all the material culture of the period. Some of this was military issue; uniform, musket, bayonet, cartridge box, belts, haversack, knapsack and canteen. Other items, obtained by the soldier individually, or perhaps issued by the military, were obtained from civilian vendors and did not differ from the items available to the general population. This group of items includes razors, combs, writing materials, eating utensils, gaming equipment, etc. The documentation available only lists the items. Type and style is open to conjecture.

HAVERSACKS (FIGURE 7C)

The Williamsburg records show material was issued for haversacks and they were undoubtedly carried by the soldiers throughout the war. The haversack served as the soldier's pocket. He kept his personal possessions in his haversack. Also, if the army was on the move, food would be cooked and kept in the haversack to eat on the march or in camp if cooking fires could not be used.

The haversack was easily constructed from a rectangular piece of linen. A fold created a bottom and the sides were sewn to create a bag. A small amount of the material remained at the top to fold over as a flap to cover the opening. The flap buttoned to the front of the bag. A strap was attached to carry the haversack slung from the shoulder.

KNAPSACKS (FIGURES 7A & B)

As with haversacks, the troops were issued material to construct knapsacks. The style of knapsacks carried by Virginians is not known. They may have had single bag or double bag models. The single bag may have been a larger version of the haversack with two straps to allow it to be

Figure 7 - Knapsacks

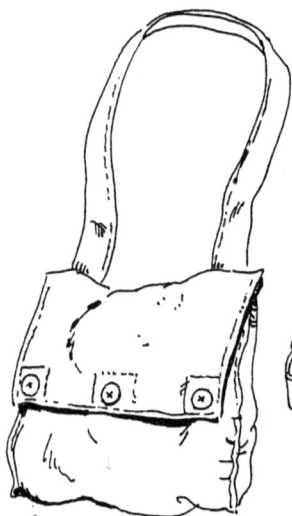

7c

7a

7b

Joe Lee
96

carried from both shoulders. It may have had one strap that allowed it to be carried slung diagonally across the back. A variation of this model has two bags connected at the top which fold against one another, the openings inside. This knapsack was slung from a single strap across the chest. The side of the knapsack exposed to the weather may have been painted to protect the contents (Klinger 1967:29-30).

If the army needed to move quickly the men might leave their knapsacks, which followed in wagons. Although they were designed so the soldier could fight while wearing his knapsack, it was often removed if action was expected. An order issued by Weedon on October 3, 1777, while trailing the British army marching in Philadelphia, calls for the men to leave their packs (knapsacks) and blankets, provisions to be carried in haversacks (Weedon 1971:74).

TENTS

The *Virginia Gazette*, October 7, 1775, had an advertisement by William Aylett, a contractor for the army, which included a request for large quantities of ducking or russia drab for tents (Goodwin 1962:8). The Williamsburg Public Store record has many references to tents from 1775-1779 (Goodwin 1962:208). As with other items, it appears that the state made an attempt to provide its troops with shelter.

References to tents usually involve the number of men assigned to each tent. General Heth, at one point, was able to provide a tent for five men (Heth 1892:340). Weedon, however, had to have eight men to each tent. It should be noted that probably two of the eight would be on guard or other duty. The common infantryman's tent of the period was six and one half feet square and five feet high (Neumann and Kravic 1975:260).

COOKWARE AND FOODSERVICE

The advertisement by William Aylett, referred to above, also calls for kettles. It specifies tin or brass (Goodwin 1962:8).

The Williamsburg Store record has many references to these items being purchased and issued (Goodwin 1962:183-185). Iron pots were not sought in the advertisement, perhaps because of the weight. The Williamsburg Store record does show, however, that iron pots were purchased and issued (Goodwin 1962:184).

The kettles came in various sizes. The ideal, it seems, was a two-gallon size that would feed six men (Jefferson 3, 1951:240, 302). Evidence that kettles continued to be used throughout the war is confirmed by Weedon (Weedon 1971:20, 219).

Kettles appear to be the only issued item connected with food consumption and preparation. There is only one reference to forks and spoons being issued from Williamsburg and that is to an artillery company (Goodwin 1962:143). These items, and also, plates, cups, and bowls, if used, were the soldier's responsibility. This, undoubtedly, resulted in a great diversity among these items.

CANTEENS

The Aylett advertisement calls for canteens and they were issued from the Williamsburg Store (Goodwin 1962:8, 160, 161). Canteens were commonly made of wood: however, tin was the standard issue for the British army. Glass bottles may have been used and possibly covered with leather or other material for protection.

BLANKETS

Blankets were an item provided by the state. Blankets are mentioned in the Williamsburg record and in the Philadelphia Public Store record as issued to every regiment of the Virginia Line (Goodwin 1962:168-172; PPS 1778-1779:9, 12-25). The blankets were probably a variety of colors and styles depending on the source and the material available to the manufacturer.

RAZORS AND COMBS

These items were shipped from Williamsburg and made available through the Philadelphia Store (Goodwin 1962:148-149; PPS 1778-1779:9, 12-25). The combs were made of horn, ivory, bone, tortoiseshell, brass, pewter, and close grain wood (Neumann and Kravic 1975:89). It can be assumed that these items were issued to the soldier with an end use in mind, although the frequency of the use is questionable. The Light Infantry Orderly Book recorded,

> ...the soldiers who mount guard coming on guard with long beards and unpowdered and other the powder slovenly put on... (Gamble 1892:255).

CONCLUSION

The tools of war used by the Virginians in the American Revolution suggest a concern for function and simplicity. Their design seems oriented to the task and avoids the decoration common to the equipment of the European soldier, products of a militaristic system. The individual pieces of equipment used by the Virginians were a direct result of the limited resources of the state, the immediate need of the troops, and other cultural factors. Although the equipment used during the Revolution was a result of these factors, it is important to note that much of the postwar equipment retained similar, if not identical characteristics. The simplicity of American military equipment remained as economics, religion, and other aspects of the American culture changed.

This simplicity is best seen in the main tool of war, the weapon. In this case, the weapon most familiar to the Virginian was the imported French musket. The French musket became the model for the American M1795, the first firearm developed and produced by the American military (Lewis 1956:46). This style was continued in American military arms throughout the nineteenth century with technological advances such as the caplock, rifled barrel, graduated rear sight, and breech-loading mechanism, being incorporated into the basic design. Although the operation of the French musket was identical to other weapons of this period, it had many features that suggest that function dictated the form.

The barrel of the musket was secured to the stock with bands rather than pins used on the English gun. This system allowed for less wood in the musket's forestock. The bands could be removed by simply sliding them over the muzzle. Then, by removing a screw in the tang of the breechplug, and one lock screw, the barrel could be lifted from the stock. This operation could be easily accomplished in the field.

The same operation performed on the English musket required the removal of the barrel pins and the screw in the tang of the breechplug. The pins had to be brought above the surface of the stock to be withdrawn requiring that a punch and mallet be used with some care to drive one end of the pin to the surface. This operation was best done at an armory by a skilled worker. Removing and inserting of these pins had the potential to cause damage to the stock.

The French M1763 and later muskets had a reinforced, double throated, cock (Figure 4b). The cock was subject to repeated abuse when it struck the frizzen and the design helped resist damage. The screw that tightened the jaws of the cock to hold the flint, had a hole at its head, below the slot for a screwdriver. This allowed the jaws to be tightened with any metal rod that would fit in the hole, if a screwdriver was not available. This would well speed up the changing of a flint in battle. The English musket needed a screwdriver to tighten the jaws of the cock. Also, the cock was S-shaped (Figure 5b), thin and delicate in comparison to the French.

The relative ease of maintaining the iron furniture of the French musket compared to the brass of the English musket was discussed earlier. The design of this furniture also illustrates the functional simplicity of the French arm. The English weapon had a decorative serpentine side plate (Figure 5c), finials on the trigger guard, and a long tang on the butt plate (Figure 5d), whereas the French musket had a simple, flat side plate (Figure 4c) and rounded ends on the trigger guard and butt plate. Also, the French musket did not require ramrod pipes, as the barrel bands served this function. The English gun had an escutcheon plate (Figure 5e) on the top of the wrist portion of the stock. Identification numbers may have been engraved or stamped on this plate but it was otherwise decorative.

The smaller bore size of the French musket suggests functional considerations. A smaller bore used a smaller ball. This allowed more balls to be produced from each pound of lead. The smaller ball and bore would allow less powder to be used. The lighter weight of the individual cartridge would mean the soldier would have less weight to carry, an important factor on the march, or could carry more ammunition into battle, another important factor.

The comparison of these weapons supports the assumption that the French design was functionally superior to its English counterpart. The selection of this weapon as a model for American produced weapons might be based on this reason. Another reason might be an anti-British, pro-French attitude following the war. It must be noted, however, that the first official American musket, M1795, was adopted during a Federalist, pro-British national administration and at the time of a quasi-war with France. Also, with the adoption of the French design, the English tradition followed during the war in American musket manufacturing was completely abandoned. It appears functional concerns played a pivotal role in the selection of this design. The avoidance of decorative elements further suggests a nonmilitaristic attitude by the Americans.

Lack of decoration and functional considerations are also apparent in the clothing of the Virginia soldier. As with the musket, clothing was subject to the state's resources as applied to pressing need. Yet, the style of clothing used in the Revolution, although a result of shortages and improvisation, was retained in many cases through the War of 1812 and beyond.

The hunting shirt is covered extensively in this study. Virginia provided this garment to all the soldiers. It was constructed from durable linen from a simple pattern that did not demand expert tailoring skills. The basic garment (Figure 1) could have a cape attached to the collar that laid over the shoulders providing a double layer of fabric for added protection from the weather. One obvious advantage to this garment is that if wet it would dry faster than a wool uniform coat. Contrasting colors could be incorporated into the collar and cuffs for identification of the soldier's regiment, his rank, and special skill, such as a musician. Though it lacked the warmth of a wool coat, a wool waistcoat worn underneath would compensate for this deficiency. The hunting shirt was adequate for the weather encountered during the regular campaign season, spring through autumn. Winter limited army activities, lessening problems due to the lack of a wool coat. The hunting shirt continued to be used by the civilian population after the war, particularly on the frontier, and reappeared as a military garment in the War of 1812.

The wool uniform coats worn by Virginians (Figure 2) were probably of the same basic tailoring pattern used for uniform coats in Europe. Yet they lacked the decorative elements common to British soldiers' coats. The decorations common to the British coat included lace binding around the button holes on the collar, lapels, and cuffs. Lace was woven with a distinctive pattern unique to each regiment. There is no evidence of the use of lace on Virginia regimental coats.

Another decorative treatment employed by the British was the use of shoulder wings. These were pieces of material that covered the outside of the shoulder and upper arm. The wings were also laced. Wings identified the regiment's elite companies, the grenadiers and light infantry (Mollo 1975:190, plate 114). There is no evidence of wings on Virginia regimental coats.

The small clothes, which were the breeches and waistcoats, and shirts did not differ from the same articles of civilian clothing. This would support a nonmilitaristic attitude. The exception in this group of clothing is the use of military overalls, which were not worn by the civilian population. The overalls provided, in a single garment, the protection to the lower part of the body that required breeches and a pair of gaiters. This functional item of clothing continued in the American military through the War of 1812.

Other equipment carried by the Virginia soldier included the simple haversack, knapsack, canteen, and bayonet in a leather scabbard. These items may have had a painted regimental identification but no other decorative elements. This would also be true of the European soldier's equipment, except the knapsack made with goat skin with the hair remaining used by some British troops. The hair may have provided protection, and therefore be functional, but such a knapsack also would have been very visible against a red coat, part of a military image.

The final piece of equipment to be examined is the cartridge box. Sources used for this study did not reveal what particular model of leather cartridge box was carried by the Virginian. It is likely he used a variety of models during the war. There is no evidence that any of these boxes had decorative elements. This was not true with the European troops.

British cartridge boxes had a metal plate, that differed by regiment, fastened to the outer flap of the box. It carried the number of the regiment and other design elements. Many of these boxes also had another plate fixed to the shoulder belt. It was also marked and was worn in the middle of the chest at the point where this belt crossed with the sling, or belt, of the bayonet scabbard (Neumann and Kravic 1975:224-226).

The documentation does confirm that the Virginia troops carried a tin cartridge canister (Figure 6c). This simple rectangular container carried thirty-six cartridges and was waterproof. Although it may have presented problems for the soldier in handling the cartridges, the protection it provided against water damage of cartridges solved an ongoing problem found in poor quality leather boxes.

The equipment used by the soldier of the Virginia Line consistently shows that form was subservient to function. This fact is reinforced when the Virginian's equipment is compared to the equipment of British and German troops. This functional simplicity carried on after the war and it can be argued it continues to the present.

The Virginia soldier's equipment was just a tool for the job. By comparison, the decorative items of the European soldier suggest that image is as important as results, or at least a perception that image is related to results. The differences in the military equipment of a militaristic system and that of a military system seems to reflect the differences in the systems. If this is the case, and Morton's statement used at the beginning of this book is correct, then the colonists of British North America had developed a society that differed from the European societies they had left. Some immigrants were dissenters and many of these individuals may have been running from military abuses in their homeland. Therefore, the development of a slightly different culture might be expected.

The population of dissenters was, however, not universal and may not have been the majority. Much of British North America was made up of common English men and women. This group did not necessarily bring attitudes contrary to the British norm to the new world. What would have changed their opinion of British military ways?

There was an ongoing military need in North America. The neglect of this need by the British government forced the colonists to rely on themselves and a very nonmilitaristic militia system. This was, quite probably, a major reason for the change of, or lack of, militaristic thinking in the colonial mind. Then, when England did respond to colonial need in the final French and Indian War, the professional British regular was slaughtered in the woods of western Pennsylvania with General Edward Braddock, in 1755, and died by the score assaulting the French works at Fort Carillon (Ticonderoga), in 1758. Even the final defeat of the French in North America could not retrieve the reputation of the British military. Arrogance of British officers, subservient roles for American provincial troops, and the lack of the British army to adjust to the ways of war in the North American forest, all but destroyed any support the British system may have had among the colonists. Their disdain for militarism is then reasserted during the years prior to the Revolution with a focus on having British army garrisons in the colonies.

Any remaining favor for establishing a European militaristic system in the United States was overwhelmed by the fact that the colonists won the war. Although the American military performed well, or even brilliantly on some occasions, such as Greene's southern campaign, it would have been foolish to believe that the military system of the colonists was the sole factor responsible for the victory. National morale played a much more decisive role. The lessons that seemed to have been learned by the national leaders were those concerned with the motivation of the soldier. They seemed to have grasped the idea that understanding the reasons for the fight were perhaps more important to the American soldier than particular traditions, including those reflected in the military material culture.

Baron Von Steuben recognized this in his famous:

You tell a European soldier to do something and he does it. You tell an American soldier to do something, you tell him why, and he does it.

It seems that an often repeated theme of the American GI of World War II would have been accepted by his Revolutionary War ancestor:

Let's go get the job done and go home.

BIBLIOGRAPHY

Arnstein, Walter L.
  1976 *Britain Yesterday and Today.*
     Lexington, Mass.: D.C. Heath and Company.

Bolton, Charles Knowles
  1902 *The Private Soldier Under Washington.*
     New York: Charles Scribner's Sons.

Brown, M. L.
  1980 *The Firearm in Colonial America 1492-1792, The Impact on
     History and Technology.*
     Washington: Smithsonian Institution Press.

Brown, William L.
  1973 "The First Maryland Regimental Field Book".
     Unpublished.

Butler, David F.
  1971 *United States Firearms, The First Century 1776-1876.*
     New York: Winchester Press.

Copeland, Peter F.
  1977 *Working Dress in Colonial and Revolutionary America.*
     Contributions in American History, Number 58.
     Westport, Conn.: Greenwood Press.

Dann, John C., Ed.
  1980 *The Revolution Remembered.*
     Chicago: University of Chicago Press.

Deetz, James
  1977 *In Small Things Forgotten.*
     Garden City, NY: Anchor Press/Doubleday.

Gamble, Robert
    1892 "Orderly Book of Captain Robert Gamble".
    Collections of the Virginia Historical Society.
    New Series. Vol II. Richmond.

Gehret, Ellen J.
    1976 *Rural Pennsylvania Clothing.*
    York, PA: Liberty Cap Books.

Gill, Harold B., Jr.
    1974 *The Gunsmith in Colonial Virginia.*
    Williamsburg: The Colonial Williamsburg Foundation.

Glatthaar, Joseph T.
    1985 *The March to the Sea and Beyond.*
    New York: New York University Press.

Goodwin, Mary R. M.
    1962 "Clothing and Accoutrements of the Officers and
    Soldiers of the Virginia Forces, 1775-1780".
    Unpublished.

Greene, Nathanael
    1980 *The Papers of General Nathanael Greene. Vol II.*
    Edited by Richard K. Showman.
    Chapel Hill: University of North Carolina Press.

    1983 *The Papers of General Nathanael Greene. Vol III.*
    Edited by Richard K. Showman.
    Chapel Hill: University of North Carolina Press.

Hamilton, Edward P.
    1962 *The French and Indian Wars.*
    Garden City: Doubleday and Company.

Hanson, James A.
    1981 *The Voyageur's Sketchbook.*
    Chadron, Nebr.: The Fur Press.

Heimert, Alan
1978 *"Religion and the American Mind." Interpreting Colonial America.*
Edited by James Kirby Martin.
New York: Harper and Row.

Herndon, G. Melvin
1981 *Financing the Revolution in Virginia.*
Yorktown: The Virginia Independence Bicentennial Commission.

Heth, William
1892 "Orderly Book of Major William Heth of the Third Virginia Regiment, May 15-July 1, 1777".
Collections of the Virginia Historical Society.
New Series. Vol. II. Richmond.

Higginbotham, Don
1961 *Daniel Morgan, Revolutionary Rifleman.*
Chapel Hill: University of North Carolina Press.

1971 *The War of American Independence.*
Bloomington: Indiana University Press.

Huddleston, Joe D.
1978 *Colonial Riflemen in the American Revolution.*
York, PA: George Shumway Publisher.

Jefferson, Thomas
1951 *The Papers of Thomas Jefferson. Vols. 3 & 4.*
Edited by Julian P. Boyd.
Princton: Princeton University Press.

Keegan, John
1987 *The Mask of Command.*
New York: Viking Penguin, Inc.

Kellogg, Louise Phelps
  1916 *Frontier Advance on the Upper Ohio.*
    Madison: State Historical Society of Wisconsin.
    Heritage Books, Inc. (Bowie, MD) 1994.

Kemp, Alan
  1976 *Yorktown.*
    London: Almark Publishing Co., Ltd.

Klinger, Robert L.
  1967 *Sketchbook '76.*
    Arlington, VA: Robert L. Klinger.

Knox, John
  1980 *The Siege of Quebec.*
    Mississauga, Ont.: Pendragon House

Lefferts, Charles M.
  1971 *Uniforms of the American, British, French, and German
    Armies in the War of the American Revolution, 1775-1783.*
    Old Greenwich, Conn.: W. E. Inc.

Lesser, Charles H.
  1976 *The Sinews of Independence, Monthly Strength Reports of
    the Continental Army.*
    Chicago: University of Chicago Press.

Lewis, Berkeley R.
  1956 *Small Arms and Ammunition in the United States Service.*
    Washington: Smithsonian Institution Press.

Mollo, John
  1975 *Uniforms of the American Revolution.*
    New York: MacMillian.

Morgan, Edmund S.
1968 *"The Puritan Ethic and the Coming of the American Revolution." The Reinterpretation of the American Revolution 1763-1789.*
Edited by Jack P. Greene.
New York: Harper and Row.

Moore, Warren
1967 *Weapons of the American Revolution and Accoutrements.*
New York: Promontory Press.

Neumann, George C.
1967 *The History of Weapons of the American Revolution.*
New York: Bonanza Books.

Neumann, George C. and Frank J. Kravic
1975 *Collector's Encyclopedia of the American Revolution.*
Harrisburg: Stackpole Books.

Palmer, William P. M.D., Ed.
1968 *Calendar of Virginia State Papers and other Manuscripts. Vol. I, II, III, VIII.*
Richmond.

Peterson, Harold L.
1968 *The Book of the Continental Soldier.*
Harrisburg, PA: Stackpole.

Public Store Records
n.d. Public Store Records, Williamsburg.
Public Store Records, Philadelphia.
Microfilm Reel 635. Virginia State Library, Richmond.

Risch, Erna
1962 *Quartermaster Support of the Army, a History of the Corps.*
Quartermaster Historian's Office.
Office of the Quartermaster General. Washington, D.C.

Royster, Charles
   1979 *A Revolutionary People at War.*
   New York: W.W. Norton and Company.

Sanchez-Saavedra, E. M.
   1978 *A Guide to Virginia Military Organizations in the American Revolution, 1774-1787.*
   Richmond: Virginia State Library.

Sellers, John R.
   1978 *The Virginia Continental Line.*
   Williamsburg: The Virginia Bicentennial Commission.

Schlereth, Thomas J.
   1980 *Artifacts and the American Past.*
   Nashville: American Assoc. for State and Local History.

   1982 *Material Culture Studies in America.*
   Nashville: American Assoc. for State and Local History.

Sizer, Theodore
   1950 *The Works of Colonel John Trumbull.*
   New Haven: Yale University Press.

Smith, Page
   1976 *A New Age Now Begins.* 2 vols.
   New York: McGraw-Hill.

South, Stanley
   1977 *Method and Theory in Historical Archeology.*
   New York: Academic Press.

Stubblefield, George
   1887 "Orderly Book of the Company of Captain George Stubblefield, 5th Virginia Regt. March 3, 1776-July 10, 1776".
   Collections of the Virginia Historical Society.
   New Series. Vol. VI. Richmond.

Taliaferro, Benjamin
1980 *The Orderly Book of Captian Benjamin Taliaferro, 2nd Virginia Detachment, Charleston, South Carolina, 1780.*
Edited by Lee A. Wallace, Jr.
Richmond: Virginia State Library.

Vagts, Alfred
1959 *A History of Militarism.*
Meridian Books.

Virginia Gazette (Purdie)
#95 (Nov. 22, 1776),   #80 (Aug. 9, 1776),
#90 (Oct. 18, 1776),   #78 (July 26, 1776),
#111 (Mar.14, 1777),   #112 (Mar. 21, 1777),
#113 (Mar. 28, 1777), #116 (April 18, 1777),
#120 (May 16, 1777),   #121 (May 23, 1777),
#141 (Oct. 10, 1777), #149 (Dec. 5, 1777),
#165 (May 29, 1778).

Virginia Gazette (Dixon and Hunter)
#1271 (Dec. 16, 1775), #1277 (Jan. 27, 1776),
#1338 (April 4, 1777).

Ward, Christopher
1952 *The War of the Revolution.* 2 Vols.
New York: MacMillian.

Washington, George
1932-1937 *The Writings of George Washington.* Vol. 7-18.
Edited by John C. Fitzpatrick.
Washington: U.S. Government Printing Office

1961 George Washington Papers.
Presidential Papers Microfilm. Series 4, Reels 46, 53, 60, 61, 62.
Washington: Library of Congress.

Weedon, George
    1971 *Valley Forge Orderly Book of General George Weedon.*
        Eyewitness accounts of the American Revolution,
            Series III.
        Arno Press.

Wright, John Womack
    1963 *Some Notes on the Continental Army. New Windsor
    Cantonment.*
        Publication No. 2.
        Cornwallville N.Y.: Hope Farm Press.

Wright, Robert K.
    1986 *The Continental Army.*
        Center of Military History.
        Washington: United States Army.

INDEX

www.ingramcontent.com/pod-product-compliance
Lightning Source LLC
Chambersburg PA
CBHW071942100426
42737CB00046BA/1914